THE SPANISH
INQUISITION
in World History

Richard Worth

Enslow Publishers, Inc.

40 Industrial Road   PO Box 38
Box 398   Aldershot
Berkeley Heights, NJ 07922   Hants GU12 6BP
USA   UK

http://www.enslow.com

Library of Congress Cataloging-in-Publication Data

Worth, Richard.
    The Spanish Inquisition in world history / Richard Worth.
       p. cm. — (In world history)
    Summary: Examines the events that led to the persecution of accused heretics against the Catholic Church, focusing on the Inquisition in medieval Spain.
    Includes bibliographical references and index.
    ISBN 0-7660-1825-3
    1. Inquisition—Spain—Juvenile literature. 2. Spain—Church history—Juvenile literature. [1. Inquisition—Spain. 2. Spain—Church history.]
    I. Title. II. Series.
    BX1735 .W67   2002
    272'.2'0946—dc211
                                                    2001008516

Printed in the United States of America

10 9 8 7 6 5 4 3 2 1

To Our Readers:
We have done our best to make sure all Internet Addresses in this book were active and appropriate when we went to press. However, the author and the publisher have no control over and assume no liability for the material available on those Internet sites or on other Web sites they may link to. Any comments or suggestions can be sent by e-mail to comments@enslow.com or to the address on the back cover.

Illustration Credits: Enslow Publishers, Inc., pp. 4, 69, 85; Gustave Doré, *Doré's Illustrations of the Crusades* (Mineola, N.Y.: Dover Publications, Inc., 1997), pp. 25, 55; Hulton Archive/Getty Images, pp. 7, 14, 18, 87, 92, 97; J.G. Heck, ed., *Heck's Pictorial Archive of Military Science, Geography and History* (New York: Dover Publications, Inc., 1994), pp. 21, 29, 30, 59, 62, 64, 67, 82, 94, 101; Reproduced from the Collections of the Library of Congress, pp. 42, 103.

Cover Illustration: © Digital Vision, Ltd. All Rights Reserved (Background); J.G. Heck, ed., *Heck's Pictorial Archive of Military Science, Geography and History*, New York: Dover Publications, Inc., 1994 (Portrait of monk).

Contents

1 Battling Heresy. 5

2 Origins of the Inquisition 12

3 Medieval Spain. 35

4 Torquemada. 48

5 Inquisitor-General 57

6 The Growth of the
   Inquisition. 76

7 Power, Decline, and Fall. 90

8 The Inquisition in History . . . 99

   Timeline 105

   Chapter Notes. 107

   Further Reading and
   Internet Addresses. 110

   Index. 111

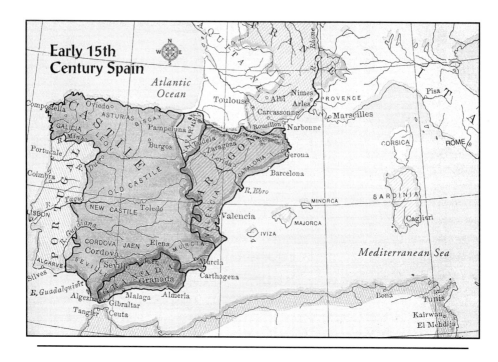

When the Spanish Inquisition started, Spain consisted of four kingdoms: Castile, Aragon, Navarre, and Granada. With their marriage in 1469, Ferdinand of Aragon and Isabella of Castile had united their two Christian kingdoms. Navarre was a small Christian kingdom in the north. Granada, in the south, was ruled by Spanish Muslims called Moors.

Chapter 1

Battling Heresy

In 1490, Benito García was hauled in front of the Spanish Inquisition. The Inquisition had been set up to expose people who had recently become Christians but might not be true to their new faith. García was a Jew who had converted to Christianity. But the Inquisition had received word that he had fallen back into Judaism, the religion of the Jews, and was practicing his old religion in secret. Therefore, it accused him of heresy—betraying the religious teachings of Christianity. At first, García denied everything. The Inquisition ordered that he receive two hundred lashings with a whip as well as other torture. Eventually, García admitted that he was guilty of practicing Judaism. However, the Inquisition was not entirely satisfied. García was also expected to name other heretics so they, too, might be punished.[1]

García mentioned the names of others. One of them was Juan de Ocaña, who had presumably led García back into Judaism. He also gave the Inquisition the names of Yucé Franco and his eighty-year-old father, both Jews. All of these men were immediately arrested and thrown into prison at Segovia, located in central Spain. While he was in prison, Yucé Franco became deathly ill. He asked to see a doctor as well as a rabbi. The Inquisition agreed, but instead of a rabbi they sent a member of the Inquisition who was dressed to look like a real holy man named Rabbi Abraham. Since he thought he was dying, Franco told the disguised Inquisitor that he had been involved in the murder of a Christian boy.

For years, Jews had been falsely accused of committing terrible acts against Christians. Among the accusations was that Jews kidnapped Christian children and nailed them to crosses, as Jesus Christ had been crucified. Jews were also reported to have removed the heart from each of these children and used the hearts to cast a spell that would protect them from the terrors of the Inquisition.

The Inquisitor-General

When the information Franco revealed was reported to the Inquisitors, they realized it was extremely important. Immediately, they sent word to Tomas de Torquemada. He was the Inquisitor-General, in charge of the Inquisition in Spain. The steely-eyed, seventy-year-old Torquemada had dedicated himself not only to eliminating heresy but to expelling every Jew from Spain. This case, involving the murder of a child, might give him the ammunition he needed to convince the Spanish monarchs, Ferdinand and Isabella, to order the expulsion of the Jews. They had hesitated to take this step because Jews filled important positions in the government. Some were wealthy bankers who loaned money to the monarchy. They

This drawing from a fifteenth century anti-Jewish text depicts Jews with a Christian boy tied to a cross. For years, Jews had been falsely accused of killing Christian children and using the blood for religious purposes.

also held important positions in Spain as shop owners, teachers, and philosophers.

Torquemada himself decided to supervise the case of Franco and García. After further questioning, Yucé Franco admitted that he had gone to the town of La Guardia in central Spain where he met several men who had talked about crucifying a Christian boy. But he refused to say any more. When asked to admit what he had told the Rabbi Abraham, Franco denied having said anything about his own involvement in the murder. Therefore, he was left in solitary confinement by the Inquisitors. This was a form of torture, and the Inquisitors hoped it would persuade him to change his story.

In the cell below Franco was Benito García. Franco heard his voice, and the two men began talking through the floorboards. During their conversations, García admitted that he was still a Jew and proud of his religion, and that he never intended to return to Christianity. These words were overheard by the Inquisitors, who were listening to them. The Inquisitors had vowed to condemn every unreformed heretic to burn at the stake.

Once again, Franco was taken into the court of the Inquisition and questioned. Eventually, he told the Inquisitors that the heart of a Christian boy had been used by several men to cast a spell. But he could tell the Inquisitors no more and was sent back to jail. Franco hated solitary confinement. So, when the Inquisitors brought him out again, he was prepared to tell them

Source Document

At a place named Inmestar, situated between Chalcis and Antioch in Syria, the Jews were amusing themselves in their usual way with a variety sports. In this way they indulged in many absurdities, and at length impelled by drunkenness they were guilty of scoffing at Christians and even Christ himself; and in derision of the cross and those who put their trust in the Crucified One, they seized a Christian boy, and having bound him to a cross, began to laugh and sneer at him. But in a little while becoming so transported with fury, they [whipped] the child until he died under their hands. . . .[2]

Stories of Jews killing Christian boys had been circulating for almost a thousand years before the Spanish Inquisition. The above story is recounted in the 5th Century Ecclesiastical History *by Socrates Scholasticus. Historians believe these stories were invented by people who had anti-Jewish feelings.*

anything. However, he asked that they spare him and his eighty-year-old father. The Inquisitors agreed.

Yucé Franco explained that the men he had mentioned to Rabbi Abraham had not only said they had crucified the boy but had actually showed Franco the boy's heart. He had no way of knowing whether this was true. In fact, historians believe that no boy was ever crucified. The men mentioned by Franco included Benito García, Ocaña, and others who had already been brought into custody by the Inquisition.

Later, the Inquisitors questioned Franco's father and tortured him. He confirmed everything his son had said, adding that he had seen the boy crowned with thorns, just as Jesus Christ had been, and crucified. The other men were tortured and admitted that they had participated in the crucifixion. But they did not implicate Franco. However, the Inquisitors were not satisfied. They wanted to condemn everyone. Only under persistent questioning and probably the threat of more torture did the murderers say that Franco had acted with them.

Torquemada had not been able to do the questioning himself. As Inquisitor-General, his duties had taken him elsewhere. But he was pleased with the outcome his Inquisitors had achieved. Not only had they uncovered heresy, but they had also exposed these Jews as murderers. The Inquisitor-General hoped he could use this information to convince the Spanish monarchs to expel all the Jews. He believed this was the only way to safeguard the Church in Spain. With the Jews gone and all the heretics imprisoned or burned, Torquemada felt Christianity would triumph.

The Fate of the Captives

Historians do not believe a boy was ever crucified at La Guardia. The entire incident may have been

Source Document

Yucé Franco, citizen and resident of Templeque in the district of Toledo, seduced Christians into his religion by telling them that the Christian religion was false and that Judaism was the true religion. And he crucified a Christian child with other Jews and Christians in recollection of the Passion of our Redemptor, Jesus Christ, and cursed Him, denying His divinity. And he participated in magic rites with the heart of the said child and with a consecrated host so that the inquisitors and all Christians would die of [disease].[3]

An Inquisitor read this proclamation to the public the day that Yucé Franco, Franco's father, Benito García, and Juan de Ocaña were all burned at the stake.

manufactured by the Inquisitors to whip up hatred against Jews and heretics. Nevertheless, the men accused of the crucifixion, including Benito García and Juan de Ocaña, were burned at the stake. Yucé Franco and his father were burned, too, even though the Inquisitors had promised otherwise. This was the fate that awaited thousands of people found guilty by the Spanish Inquisition and the Inquisitor-General, Tomas de Torquemada.

Chapter 2

Origins of the Inquisition

The Inquisition did not begin in Spain during the fifteenth century with Tomas de Torquemada. Its key element, religious persecution, started much earlier.

The Christian religion began with the life and teachings of Jesus Christ during the first century A.D. Christ himself was a victim of persecution. Eventually, he was dragged before Pontius Pilate, the Roman governor of Judea. Pilate was afraid that Christ's teachings represented a threat to the Roman government. Therefore, he condemned Jesus to be crucified on a cross in Jerusalem (in present-day Israel). Following the crucifixion, the leadership of Christianity fell to Simon Peter, one of Christ's disciples. Peter traveled throughout the Middle East, spreading the word of Christianity to anyone who would listen to him. Then he went to Rome, the center of the ancient world. In approximately A.D. 64, Peter was crucified, possibly as part of a persecution of Christians by the emperor Nero. The emperor tried to blame the Christians for setting a fire that destroyed much of Rome.

Persecutions Against the Early Christians

The early Christians were regularly singled out for persecution by the Roman government for a variety of reasons. The Christians kept themselves apart from Roman religious sects. The Christians often worshiped in secret, and their churches remained hidden to avoid persecution by the Roman authorities. This angered Roman officials. They feared that the Christians might be trying to undermine the power and religion of the empire.

There is no question that early Christians represented a challenge to Roman society. The Christians openly criticized the Roman religious beliefs. They refused to participate in the pagan (non-Christian) religious rituals that were approved by the Roman state. The Roman emperor regarded himself not only as head of the government but as chief priest of the Roman religion. Therefore, the attitudes of the early Christians presented a threat to his power. As the empire grew older, it was pressured by large tribes in western Europe and Asia Minor. They wished to control lands under Roman rule. Eventually, these tribes began to defeat the Roman legions and push back the boundaries of the empire. As defeats occurred, many

Around A.D. 36, St. Stephen became the first Christian martyr. (A martyr is someone who dies for or because of what he or she believes in.) He was stoned to death in Jerusalem.

Romans blamed the Christians, who openly scoffed at traditional religion and neglected the old gods.

Persecution of Christians occurred during the second century under the emperors Hadrian and Commodus. In A.D. 250, the emperor Decius ordered that all Romans should make sacrifices to the gods approved by the state. When many Christians refused, they were imprisoned or killed. In fact, Origen, a Christian leader in Rome, died while he was in prison. Seven years later, under the emperor Valerian, another massive persecution began throughout the empire. Christians were prohibited from attending their churches, under penalty of death. Their property was confiscated by the Roman government, and several church leaders lost their lives. The persecution finally stopped when Valerian was killed in a military campaign and succeeded by a more tolerant emperor.

The worst persecutions against the Christians began in A.D. 303 under the emperor Diocletian. He ordered the complete destruction of Christian churches and the mass burning of Christian books. Roman officials tortured Christian believers in an attempt to force them to give up their religious beliefs. Those who refused to change were killed.

The Growth of Christianity

Even in the face of persecution, Christianity continued to spread throughout the Roman Empire. As historian Kenneth Scott Latourette has pointed out, "Christianity was predominantly urban. It moved along the trade routes from city to city."[1] By the second and third centuries, Christianity had won more and more converts. With the decay of the empire, many Romans sought comfort in a new religion. Often they turned to Christianity, which had strong congregations—made even stronger by the need to withstand persecution. Many Romans were impressed by the values of the Christians. "They cared for their poor," Latourette wrote, "and for those of their number imprisoned for their faith. In times of distress churches would help one another by gifts of money or food."[2] By contrast, followers of the traditional Roman religion could not receive such support.

Christianity offered a simple message: Love God and love one another. This appealed to people of all classes. For those who followed Christ's teachings, Christianity also promised immortality. This looked increasingly attractive in a world beset by violence and destruction.

Over the years, the Church had developed a strong structure. There were individual churches where Christians could find friendship with other believers. In major cities such as Rome, Carthage in northern Africa, and Antioch in the Middle East, there were strong bishops. These were the leaders of Christianity, elected by church officials. Each bishop of Rome was considered part of an unbroken line from Simon Peter and increasingly regarded himself the head of the Church, or pope. He was selected by leading members of the Church.

Constantine and Christianity

The future of Christianity was assured by the emperor Constantine during the fourth century A.D. Constantine was struggling for control of the Roman Empire against a powerful rival, Maxentius. Before the start of the decisive battle at the Milvian Bridge near Rome in 312, Constantine reportedly saw a cross in the sky with the inscription "Conquer by this." He also said that God had appeared to him in a dream.[3]

After Constantine won the battle and took control of the empire, he granted religious tolerance to the Christians. In addition, his children were instructed in the teachings of Christianity. Christian bishops became members of his court. According to historian C. W. Previte-Orton, Constantine "decreed that the Christian churches could receive by gift . . . anything from anybody, an unexampled privilege which no [other church] had ever enjoyed. The result was that wealth flowed into them. . . ."[4] Constantine also built Christian churches in Rome as well as in his new capital city at Constantinople (now Istanbul, Turkey) in Asia Minor. He later converted to Christianity.

Constantine had brought Christianity under the special protection of the Roman state. The government permitted no disagreement with its laws. Thus, the emperor believed that devout Christians should also abide by a strict set of teachings. As a result, he called a religious council at Nicaea in Asia Minor in 324 to establish the official doctrines of the Church. The council was attended by important bishops from

Constantine was the first Roman Emperor to become Christian. After he held the Council of Nicea in 324, the Catholic Church began to root out heretics.

across the Roman world—Africa to Asia Minor. From the meetings at the Christian gathering came the Nicene Creed, the first formal definition of the faith. Among other things, the Creed declared that there were three parts of one God—the parts, called the holy trinity, consisted of: God, the father; Jesus Christ, who was the son of God; as well as God, the Holy Spirit. The Nicene Creed emphasized that all three parts of God had existed from the beginning of the world.

Dealing with Heresy

A major purpose of the Council of Nicaea was to set down the orthodox teachings of the Christian church. Orthodox Christian believers were known as Catholics. The council also wanted to eliminate a set of religious beliefs called Arianism. These had been developed by Arius, a priest in Alexandria, Egypt. Arius taught that God the father had created Jesus Christ, adding that "the Son has a beginning but that God is without beginning," and that Jesus was separate from God.[5] Although Arius had many followers, high church officials as well as the emperor Constantine believed his teachings threatened the unity of the Church. The emperor ordered that any of Arius's followers should be put to death for disobeying the Council of Nicaea. All their books were ordered to be burned. Arius himself was banished from the Church.

Arianism was considered heresy in the Catholic Church. The word *heresy* comes from a Greek word that literally means "a type of philosophy". Among church leaders, heresy meant a philosophy that disagreed with the teachings of orthodox Catholicism and, therefore, seemed to threaten the unity of the Church.

Christianity had often been the victim of persecution in the past. Now that it was powerful, it found itself persecuting others who disagreed with church doctrine. The popes were leaders in stamping out heresy. Roman emperors who embraced Catholicism, like Constantine, also regarded heresy as a threat not only to the Church but to the Roman state because its unity and power might be undermined. "The . . . contemporaries of Constantine were not wrong in saying that he had carried through a huge religious . . . revolution. To change the religion of the Roman empire was to change the world."[6]

The Rise of the Catholic Church

Following the reign of Constantine, the power of the Roman Empire in western Europe continued to decline. Meanwhile, the prestige of the Catholic Church and the pope increased. During the fifth century, perhaps the most famous pope was Leo I, who reigned from 440 to 461. Leo worked tirelessly to stamp out heresies and to assert the power of the pope over the Christian world. He faced his greatest challenge when Attila the Hun threatened to destroy

Pope Leo I successfully convinced the Huns (pictured) to spare Rome from destruction.

Rome. Attila led his tribal warriors against northern Italy in 452. Leo met with Attila and persuaded him to retreat from the city. This greatly enhanced the pope's reputation as a powerful leader.

During the sixth century, the Roman Empire's claim to its former western lands was briefly revived under the emperor Justinian, who reigned from 527 to 565. He ruled from the capital at Constantinople. Justinian built many Catholic churches across the empire, including Saint Sophia, a large cathedral in Constantinople. He also tried to root out heresy in the church by ordering a great council at Constantinople in 553 to reassert orthodox Catholic beliefs. The emperor ordered that any heretics should be killed and their property confiscated.

Following the death of Justinian, the Roman Empire collapsed in the West. Only the Catholic Church survived as a centralized institution in western Europe. Rome sent out missionaries to Germany, France, Spain, and England to convert those that they considered pagan tribes. Monasteries were established in areas as far away as Ireland, Scotland, and Egypt. The missionaries who lived there and were often called monks supported themselves by growing their own food and tending flocks of animals. While the monasteries were considered religious communities, they were also among the only centers of learning in western Europe. There was no printing press at the time. The monks made handwritten copies of some of the great books of the ancient world and preserved this information during the Middle Ages when libraries were destroyed by the invasions of pagan tribes.

The Rise of Islam and the Crusades

While Christianity was trying to maintain itself in western Europe, it faced an even more powerful threat in the Middle East. Here, the prophet Muhammad established a new religion, Islam, during the early seventh century. At the center of Islam are the beliefs written in a holy book called the Koran. These are considered to be the words of God, or Allah, to his prophet Muhammad. Islam contains five central requirements, called pillars. These include belief in unity of Allah and his prophet, Muhammad; giving money to the needy; fasting during the month of Ramadan; praying five times a day; and making a pilgrimage to Mecca, Saudi Arabia, at least once. Believers are also expected to attend services at their mosque or place of worship.

Followers of Islam, called Muslims, believed in spreading their religion throughout the world. After Muhammad's death in 632, his followers began to conquer vast areas of the Mediterranean world. Muslims captured Jerusalem in 637. This city was important to both Christianity and Islam. It is where Christ died and where Muslims believe Muhammad ascended into heaven. The Muslim armies then overran much of North Africa and crossed the eastern Mediterranean to conquer Spain during the eighth century.

The Catholic Church regarded Islam as the greatest threat to its future because certain Muslims threatened to conquer Christian kingdoms and destroy Christianity. But there was little the pope could do to roll back the Islamic tide. He was a spiritual leader and did not have a large army to put in the field. Gradually, strong leaders began to emerge in western Europe. They consolidated small kingdoms in France, England, and Germany. These were rulers who recognized the pope as the leader of Christendom—the areas of Europe that believed in Christianity. They might undertake a great campaign against the Muslims if the pope asked them. The pope alone headed Europe's largest institution, one that offered believers the promise of eternal life if they defended Christian principles against heretics such as the Muslims.

In 1095, Pope Urban II called a council in Clermont, France, where he announced a great crusade. This was a holy war to retake Jerusalem and other cities from the Muslims. Many rulers responded to the pope's call. In part, they saw themselves as participating in a great religious campaign carrying out God's will to destroy the infidels, the nonbelievers. But these men also agreed to participate in the crusade because they hoped to enrich themselves with new lands in the Middle East. The First Crusade was led by French noblemen such as Count Raymond of Toulouse, Duke Robert of Normandy, and Godfrey of Bouillon. In 1098, they captured Antioch in the

The Christian victory at the Battle of Antioch was a turning point of the First Crusade.

Middle East from the Muslims. In the following year, they retook Jerusalem. The crusaders held Jerusalem during much of the twelfth century. Then it was recaptured by the great Muslim leader Saladin. The popes then called additional crusades, which headed east to fight the Muslims. But these military campaigns were unsuccessful in retaking Jerusalem.

The Crusading Spirit in Western Europe

Meanwhile, the popes began to apply the same crusading spirit in western Europe. They wanted to root out heretics who were challenging the Church. Among these heretics were the Albigensians who had arisen around Albi, a town in southern France. In this area, many church leaders were corrupt, openly taking mistresses and living in luxury while many of their parishioners were poor. The Albigensians vowed to cleanse the Church. They opposed the authority of the pope in Rome and disagreed with some of the Church's teachings.

Pope Innocent III, who reigned from 1198 to 1216, called on French leaders, including the Count of Toulouse, to step in and put down these heresies. When the count did nothing, Pope Innocent decided to send a representative, Peter of Castelnau, to talk to the Albigensians. Peter was murdered, giving Innocent a reason to call a crusade to put down the Albigensians.

The Crusade continued during much of the thirteenth century until the Albigensians were destroyed. Their lands were also seized. As the crusaders entered one of their strongholds, a representative of the pope ordered them to destroy everyone, whether heretic or devout Christian. Do not try to decide whom to spare, he said: "Kill them all, for God knows His own" and would give the true believers eternal life.[7]

In addition to waging war against the Albigensians, the pope sent in church officials, called clergy, to preach against heresy. Among them were the Order of Friars Preachers, or Dominicans. The order was founded by a Spaniard, Dominic Guzman, in 1217. Guzman established a small community of friars in Toulouse, in southern France. From this base they preached among the heretics and hoped to win them over with love and holiness, as well as a vow of poverty. Gradually, Dominicans also entered universities in Paris and Bologna, Italy. Here they became renowned teachers. By 1277, there were over four hundred Dominican houses in Europe.

In 1218, Dominic Guzman traveled to Rome, where he met another great religious leader, Francis of Assisi. Francis had founded a religious order, called the Franciscans, in 1209. Originally, the Franciscans took a vow of poverty, giving up all earthly belongings and going among the poor to preach the word of God. After Francis died in 1226, the Franciscan order changed. The Franciscans became more worldly, opening many new religious houses and acquiring large financial gifts from wealthy people. Some of the Franciscans also entered universities, where, like the Dominicans, they became teachers. The influence of the Franciscans and Dominicans also began to grow in Rome, where they served as counselors to the pope.

The Beginning of the Inquisition

In 1231, Pope Gregory IX called on the Franciscans and Dominicans to undertake a special role in the Church. They were to root out heretics as part of the papal Inquisition. The word *inquisition* comes from the Latin verb *inquiro*, meaning "to investigate." The Inquisitors were dispatched throughout western Europe to seek out people who were accused of heresy. Most of the Inquisitors were Franciscan or Dominican friars. Some historians believe that Pope Gregory may have been trying to assert control by Rome over other efforts to deal with heresy.

In the past, mobs of unruly townspeople had sometimes taken matters into their own hands. They had burned supposed heretics at the stake without first holding a trial. In 1114, for example, a mob in Beauvais, France, removed heretics from a prison and took them out to be burned. Between 1183 and 1206, Bishop Hugo of Auxerre in France exiled some heretics and had others burned. In other cases, local government officials had condemned heretics to the stake.

Beginning in 1231, special Inquisitors began to preside at trials involving alleged heretics. In 1232, the Dominicans were sent to Germany, Spain, and Lombardy (in Italy). In 1233, they went to Auxerre,

Most Inquisitors were Franciscan (pictured) or Dominican friars.

During the beginning of the Inquisition, Dominican (center) and Franciscan friars were sent to various parts of Europe to route out heretics.

Bourges, Bordeaux, and Narbonne in France. By 1255, the Inquisition was operating across western Europe.

The Inquisitors usually followed a fixed procedure. They arrived in a specific area and gave the inhabitants a month's "term of grace" in which to come before the Inquisitors and willingly confess their heresy. Then the repentant heretics were given a penance, or punishment for their sin. This might include a pilgrimage to a holy shrine, a public whipping, or a fine. Those who were believed to be heretics but who did not confess were put on trial before the Inquisitors. The accused was forced to testify against himself or herself and was not given the help of any legal counsel. A heretic was not even allowed to face witnesses who had accused him or her of heresy, nor was he or she told their names. Frequently, the Inquisitors took the word of disreputable criminals or heretics against an accused person. If the supposed heretic still did not confess, the Inquisitors might resort to torture to induce a confession. If the torture was successful and the heretic confessed, he or she could then put a hand on the Bible, kneel, and renounce his or her heresy. The confessed heretic then would have to serve out his or her penance. Heretics who still did not confess were condemned to burn at the stake.

One of the best-known Inquisitors was a Dominican friar named Bernard Gui. He was born about 1261 and joined the Dominican Order in 1279. Gui became an Inquisitor in 1307 and operated out

Source Document

Driven out of his mind by anger, the inquisitor ordered that . . . the prisoner be put first in a bath of hot water, then of cold. Then, with a stone tied to his feet, he was raised up again [by a pulley attached to the high roof of the house], kept there for a while, and dropped again, and his shins were poked with reeds as sharp as swords. Again and again he was hauled up until, on the thirteenth elevation, the rope broke and he fell from a great height with the stone still tied to his feet. . . . he lay there only half alive, with his body shattered. The [inquisitor's] servant took the body and disposed of it in a cesspool.[8]

Torture was common during the Inquisition. This account describes a particularly cruel inquisitor's reaction to a man's refusal to admit that he was a heretic.

of Toulouse until 1324. About this time he finished writing guidelines for other Inquisitors in the procedures to follow in their work. While he was an Inquisitor, he passed sentences on at least 930 people. More than forty-five of them were condemned to die at the stake. This sentence was not carried out by the Church, which was not permitted to violate the commandment against taking human life.

Source Document

[Inquisitor]. Will you then swear that you have never learned anything contrary to the faith which we hold to be true?

[Accused]. (Growing pale) If I ought to swear, I will willingly swear.

[Inquisitor]. I don't ask whether you ought, but whether you will swear.

[Accused]. If you order me to swear, I will swear.

[Inquisitor] I don't force you to swear, because as you believe oaths to be unlawful, you will transfer the sin to me who forced you; but if you will swear I will hear it.

[Accused]. Why should I swear if you do not order me to?

[Inquisitor]. So that you may remove suspicion of being a heretic. . . .

. . . If one consents to swear that he is not a heretic I say to him, "If you wish to swear so as to escape the stake, one oath will not suffice for me, nor ten, nor a hundred, nor a thousand . . . Moreover, if I have, as I resume, adverse witnesses against you, your oaths will not save you from being burned. You will only stain your conscience without escaping death. But if you will simply confess your error, you may find mercy." Under this anxiety, I have seen some confess.[9]

Bernard Gui, an Inquisitor in the early fourteenth century, gives a unique insight into how an Inquisitor questions an accused heretic. From this, one can see that an Inquisitor was more interested in a person confessing to heresy than in a person denying that they ever were a heretic.

However, the Church supported this form of punishment, as long as the local government conducted the burning.

Because of the power of the Inquisitors, they were expected to be men of the highest moral character. They were supposed to be committed to purifying the Church and eliminating heresy. Unfortunately, some Inquisitors were corrupt or too eager. In Toulouse during the thirteenth century, Count Raymond VII burned heretics even though they had confessed their heresy. Individuals might also use the Inquisition to take revenge on a neighbor by falsely accusing him of heresy. A condemned heretic was then forced to give up all his wealth. Raymond's successor, Count Alphonse, manipulated the Inquisition to confiscate the lands of supposed heretics so he could increase his own domain.

Thus, there were many precedents for the Inquisition that began in Spain during the fifteenth century. However, none would exceed the Spanish Inquisition in terms of its cruelty.

Chapter 3

Medieval Spain

Spain had a long history of Christianity dating from the first century A.D. The Spanish peninsula was then part of the Roman Empire. Christians began worshiping in the Spanish cities. Gradually, over the next few centuries, the religion became popular in the countryside. During the fourth century, Spain was conquered by the Visigoths from central Europe, led by their king Ataulf. The Visigoths strongly believed in the Arian form of Christianity, while the Roman population of Spain was Catholic. In 589, at the Council of Toledo, the Visigoth leader Recared gave up Arianism and accepted Catholicism. This brought religious unity to Spain.

Nevertheless, the Visigoths were often politically divided among powerful rivals. All of them claimed the throne. During the eighth century, some of the Visigoths revolted against their king, Roderic. The rebels sought help from the Muslims in North Africa, who had conquered this area following the death of Muhammad. A small army of Muslims crossed into Spain to support the rebels. Roderic was killed in battle in 711. Spain collapsed into various factions. The following year, a much stronger army of Muslims invaded Spain. By 730, the Muslims had conquered almost the entire peninsula. They called the new Islamic kingdom Al Andalus.

Source Document

. . . if any Jew—of those, naturally, who are as yet not baptized [into the Catholic religion] or who have postponed their own or their children's baptism—should prevent his slaves from being baptized in the presence of the priest, or should withhold himself and his family from baptism, or if any one of them should exceed the duration of one year after the [enactment] of this law, the [guilty person] of these conditions . . . shall have his head shaved, receive a hundred lashes [from a whip], and pay the required penalty of exile. . . .[1]

In seventh century Spain, the ruling Visigoths persecuted the Jews. In the above document, part of the Visigothic Code, King Erwig (680–687) states that any Jews not converting to Catholicism will be whipped and cast out of Spain.

Muslims and Christians in Spain

Since Spain was far removed from the seat of Muslim power in the Middle East, it gradually became an independent state. Like the Visigoths, the Spanish Muslims, called Moors, were often divided among themselves. Periodically, a strong ruler would mount the throne and restore unity, only to be followed by civil wars. Meanwhile, the Christian leaders, who had fled to the north of Spain, were trying to push back the Moorish territories and regain them for Catholicism. During the ninth century, for example, King Alfonso III won several important victories over the Moors. As historian Jean Plaidy wrote: "This was a sign. The Christians, living their hard lives in the north, were growing stronger; the Arabs were growing weaker. . . ."[2] But Alfonso died in 910, and the Moors, under a strong leader named al-Mansūr, pushed the Christians northward once again. "It was [al-Mansūr]," explained Plaidy, "who, after a battle which brought him thirty thousand Christian prisoners, ordered them all to be decapitated, their heads and bodies piled high. . . ."[3]

Nevertheless, the Christian leaders would crusade for the next seven hundred years to reconquer Spain from the Muslims. This Crusade was led by the kings of León, a small kingdom in northern Spain. During the tenth century, they had begun to build fortified outposts against the Muslims on the Rio Ebro river. This part of Spain soon became known as Castile, the "land of castles." In the eleventh century, Castile became an independent kingdom. It was defended by knights and peasants who knew that they represented the southern defenses of Christianity against the Muslim Empire in Spain. During the eleventh century, King Ferdinand I expanded the boundaries of Castile. He forced the Moorish leaders in Seville and Toledo in central Spain to recognize him as their king.

The increasing success of the Christians was due to several factors. First, they were used to the harsh lives of warriors. Their strongholds were rough, cold fortresses. Meanwhile, in the south, the Muslims had built themselves large pleasure palaces in Cordoba, Malaga, and Seville. They had grown accustomed to lives of luxury that did not prepare them for the conditions of military campaigning. Second, populations in the Christian kingdoms were expanding, so their leaders could put more and more warriors in the field. Third, they had also developed successful agriculture in the north to feed their armies. Finally, the same crusading spirit that had sent Christians to the Middle East to reconquer Jerusalem motivated the Spanish Christians to push the Muslims out of Spain.

During the eleventh century, Alfonso VI of León captured the Moorish stronghold at Toledo. At the same time, along the eastern coast of Spain, another Christian kingdom was developing. During the twelfth century, Count Raymond-Berengar I of Barcelona in Catalonia united his lands with nearby Aragon by marrying the Aragonese queen. In addition, Aragon controlled a broad coastal area, known as Valencia.

Over the next two centuries, Aragon and Castile would become the greatest states of Spain.

In 1212, led by Alfonso VIII of Castile, the Christian knights won a great victory over the Moors at Las Navas de Tolosa in central Spain. Muslim Spain gradually grew smaller. The Christians took Seville in 1248. The Moors were confined to a small kingdom, Granada, in southern Spain.

The Growth of Aragon and Castile

With its coastline on the Mediterranean Sea, Aragon was perfectly situated to become a trading state. During the late thirteenth and early fourteenth centuries, Aragon established a merchant empire that included Sardinia, Sicily, and Naples. Aragon's ships carried spices and cloth throughout the Mediterranean to destinations as far away as Alexandria, Egypt, and the ports of Syria.

The cities of Aragon, such as Valencia and Barcelona, and the middle classes who lived in them, grew prosperous. As a result of their wealth and power, the merchants were able to develop a strong parliament, or legislature, that ruled with the king. The parliament, or *Cortes*, included representatives of the towns, clergy, and nobles. Each part of the Aragon kingdom—Aragon, Catalonia, and Valencia—had its own Cortes. The king needed the consent of the Cortes before important laws could be passed. As historian J. H. Elliott has written: "The Cortes were therefore by the end of the Middle Ages powerful and highly developed institutions which played an indispensable part in the governing of the land."[4]

Castile was quite different from Aragon. ". . . Castile was a pastoral and nomadic society, whose habits and attitudes had been shaped by constant warfare," wrote Elliott.[5] The Castilian kingdom had been at the forefront of the reconquest. Its great heroes were brave knights, called *hidalgos*, who engaged in warfare. In 1230, one of these warriors, Ferdinand III, had united Leon and Castile under one crown. Castile was dominated by powerful aristocrats who owned vast estates. Since the soil was poor, these estates did not grow many crops but raised vast herds of sheep. Thus, Castile became a major exporter of wool. From towns such as Burgos in the northern part of the kingdom, Castilian ships carried wool to Flanders in northern Europe. There the wool was woven into clothing.

Unlike Aragon, Castile did not have a strong Cortes. Instead, the aristocrats held vast power because of their enormous estates. The aristocrats regarded themselves as monarchs and they often fought with the kings of Castile for political control of the country. As a result, the kingdom regularly found itself involved in civil wars.

The Coming of Ferdinand and Isabella

During the fifteenth century, economic conditions in Aragon began to decline. The Aragonese were in competition with the merchants of Genoa in Italy for control of major markets in the Mediterranean. Gradually, the Genoese began to increase their markets

40

and push out the Aragonese. Meanwhile, the king of Aragon, Alfonso the Magnanimous, was trying to rule Aragon from his palace in Naples. As a result, the central government in Aragon grew weaker. The upper classes began to take more and more power into their own hands.

Alfonso left Aragon to be governed by his brother John, who was married to Joanna, a Castilian. In 1458, John ascended to the throne on the death of his brother. The new king and his wife were not liked by many of the people because of their dictatorial method of rule. As a result, a revolt broke out between 1462 and 1472.

In the meantime, civil war also raged in Castile. In 1468, King Henry IV, who had no male heirs, recognized the right of his sister, seventeen-year-old Isabella, to succeed him as monarch of Castile. Isabella was an attractive, very religious young woman with a strong will. Against the wishes of her brother, she had decided to marry Ferdinand. He was the son of John and Joanna of Aragon. Isabella's wish was to unite the two kingdoms and strengthen Spain. When Henry found out about his sister's decision, he threatened to imprison her. She was eventually rescued by the archbishop of Toledo and a group of his soldiers. They took her to Valladolid in north central Spain. There she was married to Ferdinand on October 19, 1469.

Almost immediately Henry decided that Isabella should not succeed him. Instead he decided to make his illegitimate daughter, Juana, his heir. When Henry IV

Ferdinand and Isabella were the monarchs who brought on the Spanish Inquisition and forced the Jews to leave Spain.

died in 1474, Isabella declared herself the queen of Castile. A year later, Juana, supported by her own armies, claimed the throne. Ferdinand now played a crucial role in the civil war that followed. Although still a young man in his early twenties, Ferdinand had already gained experience as a warrior in Aragon. He had also been trained by his father's advisors in the arts of diplomacy.

Eventually, Ferdinand and Isabella defeated the rebels. By 1479, they were in complete control of

Castile. That same year, Ferdinand's father died and he became king of Aragon. Castile and Aragon were now united.

Ruling the Kingdoms

After becoming king of Aragon, Ferdinand vowed to retain the strong parliamentary institutions, such as the Cortes. This appealed to many people who had opposed his father during the civil war. In Castile, however, the government became far more like a dictatorship. Ferdinand and Isabella decided to reduce the power of the wealthy aristocrats so they could never again challenge the power of the throne.

The monarchs relied on a central police force that patrolled the roads and reduced crime. This police force prevented local aristocrats from trying to enforce the law themselves. The royal council, or Council of Castile, became the most powerful element of the royal administration. Ferdinand and Isabella filled it with their own loyal followers, who would carry out the monarchs' wishes. The monarchs also removed the powerful aristocrats from their role in the central government. The council was the chief court of Castile, and it supervised the local courts throughout the kingdom.

In addition, Ferdinand and Isabella appointed *corregidores* to all the towns. These individuals were expected to monitor the affairs of each community to make sure it abided by the wishes of the monarchs. The corregidores, who represented the power of the central government, were also supposed to prevent the nobility from participating in local affairs.

Ferdinand and Isabella wanted to assert their authority not only over the nobility, but also over the Catholic Church in Castile. During the centuries of reconquest, the clergy had increased its power. Catholic bishops and archbishops in Castile controlled large estates where they held supreme power and could defy the power of the monarchy. Ferdinand and Isabella could not allow this situation to continue.

Gradually, the monarchs began to assert their right to determine who would be appointed bishops and archbishops in the Spanish Church. In the past, these men had been selected by local clergy acting together with the pope in Rome. Since the new bishops now owed their position to the throne, they were more likely to give it increased power over the Church's lands. Isabella was committed to ending corruption in the Church and improving the morality of local priests. She wanted to cleanse the Catholic Church of all abuses.

Dealing with the Jews

Ferdinand and Isabella were convinced that the Church could not be fully cleansed unless it dealt with the Jews. Jews believe in one God. This God is considered loving but also a power to be feared by his followers, especially if they commit wrongdoing. God expects them to follow his laws and lead holy lives. Although the Jews believe in one God, they do not regard Jesus as the son of God. Nor do they recognize Muhammad as a great prophet.

During the years that the Moors had controlled Spain, Jews were tolerated in the realm. Indeed, Jewish scholars participated in a renaissance of learning during the ninth and tenth centuries. As the Moorish Empire declined, the Jews found themselves ruled by Christian kingdoms. Jews continued to play important roles as scholars, doctors, and merchants. They were also successful bankers who lent money to the monarchies and helped finance their military campaigns.

However, the Jews were often resented for their wealth. Many Christians also regarded the Jews almost as foreigners. They had different religious beliefs, different holidays, and even different dress. Christians also blamed the Jews for the crucifixion of Christ. From time to time, this anti-Semitism—which has come to be known as the hatred of the Jews—led to violent persecution. In 1391, for example, riots broke out among Christians against the Jews, who were blamed for bringing a terrible plague to Spain that killed thousands of people. Jews were murdered, their homes were robbed, and their synagogues were burned. Approximately fifty thousand Jews were killed. Also, new laws were passed that required Jews to wear special badges that identified them as Jews. They were not allowed to marry Christians or to enter professional fields such as medicine.

To escape persecution and death, many Jews converted to Christianity. This enabled them to resume their lives without the restrictions placed on Jews who continued to follow the Jewish faith. During the fifteenth century, these recent converts, or *conversos*, as they were called, were permitted to hold high government offices. They could also serve as judges, royal tax collectors, and even hold important positions in the Church. In some cases, they replaced old Christians who had held these positions in the past.

However, the conversos were often envied for their success by Christians. The Christians believed this success would not have been possible if these former Jews had not converted to Christianity. Many Christians also suspected that the former Jews might still be carrying on their old religious practices in private. During the 1470s, a Franciscan friar named Alonso de Espina was spreading the word that the conversos were an evil influence in Spain. He accused them of starting the plague, putting poison into the drinking water, and even kidnapping Christian boys and crucifying them. He traveled throughout Spain urging that the Inquisition, which had started in the thirteenth century, should deal with the conversos.

At first, Ferdinand and Isabella were opposed to the Inquisition. It was controlled by the pope in Rome. The two monarchs wanted to reduce the power of the pope in their realm. They believed that the pope already had too much influence in the appointment of bishops. Also, the conversos had been accepted by Ferdinand and Isabella as loyal subjects. Some of them even served as advisors to the monarchs.

However, the monarchs feared that some conversos were secretly returning to their old faith. This threatened the purity of the Church. It could easily undermine the unity of a kingdom that had only recently been beset by civil strife. As historian B. Netanyahu wrote, "the struggle against the [Jews] was felt as a struggle against a foreign *nation. . . .*"[6] Indeed, during the middle of the fifteenth century, attacks had already broken out against the Jews in cities such as Toledo and Cordoba.

According to Netanyahu, Ferdinand and Isabella were also concerned about angering many Christians who did not like the Jews. After years of civil war, the two monarchs feared that new rebellions might break out if they did not take a hard line against the conversos. While trying to reduce the power of the nobles, Ferdinand and Isabella could not risk losing the support of any other Spaniards. The monarchs would need this support when they renewed the Crusade against the Muslims who still occupied southern Spain in the kingdom of Granada. All of these factors led to a harsh policy aimed against the conversos.

In 1478, Ferdinand and Isabella established a tribunal known as the Inquisition of Castile. Its job was to investigate reports of heresy among the conversos. The Inquisition was set up to put an end to heresy and return the conversos to the Christian faith. In making this fateful decision, Ferdinand and Isabella had been strongly influenced by a powerful clergyman and close friend of the queen's—Tomas de Torquemada. He would play a crucial role in making the Inquisition respected and feared throughout Spain.

Torquemada

Tomas de Torquemada was born near Valladolid in central Spain in 1420. During the fourteenth century, members of the Torquemada family had served the Castilian kings, who had made them knights of Castile. Therefore, they held an important position in Castilian society. Many Castilian nobles did not want their families to mix with Jews or conversos. However, Tomas's grandfather, Alvar de Torquemada, married a woman who was probably a convert from Judaism to Christianity.

As a child, Tomas studied hard and was devoutly religious. Eventually, he attended college and received a doctoral degree in religion and philosophy. After completing his studies, Torquemada decided to enter the Dominican Order as a friar. His uncle, Cardinal Juan de Torquemada, may have been a role model for

Tomas. Cardinal Torquemada became a Dominican at age sixteen and distinguished himself as a brilliant church scholar. He had been a prior—head—of a Dominican religious house, and later rose to a position of leadership in the Catholic Church in Spain. The cardinal was a dedicated church reformer. He devoted himself to improving the morality of Catholic priests. He was also a firm opponent of heresy. Nevertheless, Cardinal Torquemada held a very liberal position on Spanish conversos. He believed that once they had converted to Christianity, all their past sins had been forgiven. He felt these people should be left in peace. Perhaps he had been influenced by the example of his mother.

Like his uncle, Tomas became prior of a Dominican house, the Monastery of Santa Cruz in Segovia, Spain. Torquemada was a strict leader. He wore a hair shirt—a shirt made of rough animal hair worn in direct contact with the skin as a punishment for sins—under his friar's robes, refused to eat meat, and slept on a board. Indeed, Torquemada set such an example that he was selected by Isabella to be her confessor when she was still a young woman. Wealthy aristocrats and members of the royal family frequently had their own confessors. Confessors were individual priests to whom people could confess their sins and receive absolution. Absolution is the freedom to not feel guilty for committing a sin. From his position first as a Dominican prior, then as a member of the royal household and confessor to the sister of Castile's king,

Torquemada was probably aware of Castilian official policy toward the conversos and the Jews.

In 1461, for example, Henry IV had requested that the pope allow him to establish an Inquisition in Castile to eliminate heresy. Eventually, the king decided that an Inquisition might not be necessary. Investigations by his advisors showed that there were very few conversos who seemed guilty of heresy. Nevertheless, some of the leading Dominicans and Franciscans disagreed with the king's decision. One of them, a Franciscan friar named Alonso de Espina, led a religious campaign throughout Castile. He called for an Inquisition to uncover heresy among the conversos and burn heretics at the stake.

Espina's campaign may have inflamed tensions between Christians and conversos in Castile, leading to an uprising in Carmona and riots against the conversos in 1462. Several years later, the situation in Toledo became very bad. The conversos were arming themselves in anticipation of attacks by the Christians. They believed that the Christians wanted to enrich themselves by confiscating the wealth of some of the well-to-do conversos. In 1467, fighting finally broke out between Christians and conversos. Many of the conversos' homes were burned and one hundred fifty of them lost their lives.[1] Nevertheless, the conversos themselves were blamed for causing the bloodshed. Those who had held positions in the city government were removed from office and prevented from participating in Toledo politics.

Although Torquemada no longer served as Isabella's confessor after she became queen, he continued to be one of her most trusted advisors in religious affairs. As a fierce opponent of heresy, Torquemada probably supported the way the conversos were treated in Toledo. Meanwhile, another Dominican, named Alonso de Hojedo, delivered sermons accusing the conversos of Seville of still being Jews in secret.

Hojedo, along with Torquemada, strongly advised Isabella that the only way to rid Castile of heresy was to begin an Inquisition there. This, they said, "would ensure punishment" for all heretics.[2] Ferdinand also supported an Inquisition. He had experience with it in Aragon, where papal Inquisitors had begun cleansing the kingdom of heretics before its union with Castile. In addition, Ferdinand believed an Inquisition would bring financial benefits. He realized that the government could confiscate the wealth owned by the conversos who were guilty of heresy. This income would strengthen the central government, which had spent vast sums to win the civil war against Juana. Money would also be available for a war to drive the Moors out of their stronghold in Granada and remove them from the Spanish peninsula.

The Beginnings of the Inquisition

Queen Isabella knew that Torquemada strongly favored an Inquisition in Castile. Meanwhile, the queen had even received permission from Pope Sixtus IV to begin an Inquisition in 1478. Still, the queen hesitated to begin such a harsh method of dealing with the conversos. Some of them were among her chief advisors and close friends. She also knew that the conversos would strongly resist an Inquisition, which might even undermine support for the Spanish monarchy. Finally, the queen was convinced that if they could receive stronger training in the Catholic religion, the conversos might truly embrace the faith. Her position was supported by Don Pedro Gonzalez de Mendoza, the only Spanish cardinal. So the queen put Cardinal Mendoza in charge of trying to help the conversos improve their Catholic faith.

Although Torquemada opposed the queen's decision, he had no choice but to wait until Cardinal Mendoza had completed his work among the conversos. How great was the task confronting the cardinal? Queen Isabella's biographer, Nancy Rubin, explained that "some *conversos* had maintained close ties to Judaism. Many 'new' Christians still had Jewish relatives and friends. . . . others refused to abandon Judaism, but practiced it alongside their newfound Christianity."[3] Although Cardinal Mendoza tried for two years to instill Catholicism among the conversos, he failed. By 1480, it had become clear to Isabella that an Inquisition would be necessary. "To allow [heresy] to continue . . . was, to Isabella's scrupulous conscience, spiritually irresponsible," Rubin wrote, almost like "committing heresy herself."[4]

Meanwhile, the Cortes in Castile wanted Ferdinand and Isabella to strengthen laws against the Jews—those who had never converted to Catholicism. In 1480, the two monarchs agreed that Jews should be forced to live in special ghettos, away from Christians. This was a terrible humiliation for the Jews of Castile.

At the same time, Ferdinand and Isabella asked Torquemada to nominate two Inquisitors for Seville. They were Dominicans—Miguel de Morillo and Juan de San Martin. Fearing the Inquisition, many conversos in Seville left the city. Some headed to the far corners of Castile, others went to Portugal, and still others sought refuge among the Moors in Granada.

Those who remained would now be subject to the Inquisition. One of them was a wealthy converso named Diego de Susan. He refused to submit to the Inquisitors and called a meeting among other conversos to oppose the Inquisition. Their meeting was overheard by de Susan's daughter, who was in love with a Christian. She reported her father's plot to the Inquisition. De Susan and his friends were quickly rounded up, tried and convicted of heresy, and burned at the stake in 1481.

Other conversos feared they might be next. They were compelled to confess their sins to save themselves from the fires of the stake. "Twenty thousand *conversos* came forward," wrote historian Jean Plaidy, "trembling with terror, to admit that they had at times practiced Jewish rites."[5] But this was not enough. The Inquisitors told these conversos that they must prove their sincerity by turning in others who practiced Judaism in secret. Otherwise, they would still go to the stake and their families would lose all their property. Hundreds more were turned in to the Inquisition. Some admitted that they were still Jews; others were tortured until they confessed. According to one report, by the end of 1481, almost three hundred conversos in Seville had been burned at the stake. The Inquisition had unleashed all the pent-up hatred and anti-Semitism Christians felt toward the conversos.

Sixtus IV and the Inquisition

Some conversos had been fortunate enough to escape Seville ahead of the Inquisition and journeyed to Rome. There, they told Pope Sixtus IV of the abuses of the Inquisition. Angry over what was occurring in Spain, Pope Sixtus criticized the Inquisitors for being far too harsh. He said that many people had been wrongly accused of heresy, had been tortured mercilessly, and had had their property confiscated unfairly. In 1482, he appointed a Supreme Council of eight Dominicans to direct the Spanish Inquisition. Among them was Torquemada, whom the pope considered an honest and dedicated man. By this time, Torquemada had become the confessor to King Ferdinand, so his influence over the monarchy had grown even stronger.

Both Isabella and Ferdinand agreed that a man of Torquemada's honesty and religious purity should be appointed to head the entire Inquisition. According to

By order of Pope Sixtus IV, representatives from the Roman Catholic Church collect taxes to fund the crusades. Though the pope also gave his approval for an Inquisition in Spain, he found the treatment of the accused before 1482 too harsh.

Rafael Sabatini, Torquemada's biographer, he had gained a reputation over many years for "sincerity," "sanctity," and "rigid purity."[6] Therefore, they asked the pope to appoint Torquemada to direct the entire Inquisition in Spain. Late in 1483, at age sixty-three, Torquemada was named Inquisitor-General for Castile as well as for Aragon. These states had not yet been formally united as one political unit.

Meanwhile, Ferdinand and Isabella had decided that another way to deal with the problem of the conversos was to remove the Jews from Castile. They were convinced that the Jews were persuading conversos to practice Judaism privately. If the Jews were no longer there, the conversos might become more devout Christians. In 1483, the monarchs ordered that all the Jews living in Castile must leave the kingdom. Historians do not know whether Torquemada had any influence over this decision, but he no doubt agreed with it.

In the decade that followed, Torquemada would try to complete the job of removing all remaining Jews from Spain. He would devote himself to rooting out any remaining Catholic heretics and cleansing the Catholic Church.

Inquisitor-General

Once Torquemada had been appointed Inquisitor-General, he established courts of the Inquisition throughout Castile. These courts met in Seville, Cordoba, Jaén, and Toledo. Any Inquisitors who were not prepared to recognize the authority of Torquemada were immediately dismissed and replaced with men loyal to the Inquisitor-General. Torquemada also called a meeting in Seville on October 29, 1484, to formalize the rules that should guide the Inquisition. Torquemada and his associates produced twenty-eight guidelines, which were called his "instructions."

The instructions reflected the dedication of Torquemada to the goal of eliminating heresy in Spain. The tall, thin, elderly Inquisitor had a religious fervor that "burned through every inch" of him, fueled

The Spanish Inquisition

by "his hatred of Jews and conversos."[1] While the instructions were based on the work of earlier Inquisitors such as Bernard Gui, Torquemada went further in refining the methods for dealing with heretics.

According to the instructions, after the Inquisitors arrived in a community, they were expected to give everyone guilty of heresy a period of grace lasting thirty to forty days in which to come forward and confess their sins. These sinners would be given a minimal penance, such as a fine, and permitted to resume their lives. Those who waited to come forward until after the grace period would be dealt with far more harshly. All their property would be confiscated, and they might even be sent to prison for a life sentence.

Children were encouraged to save themselves by turning in parents or relatives suspected of being heretics. Thus, a child was expected to betray his parents. This created a terrible atmosphere within families. Parents who might have been practicing Jewish religious customs were constantly afraid of being reported to the Inquisition by their own children.

Individuals who had been reported might not even be aware of it until a knock came at their door, usually in the middle of the night. Then they would be confronted by the soldiers employed by the Inquisition. To prevent accused individuals from screaming, they were often gagged. One type of gag was "shaped like a pear. It could be enlarged by means of screws, and was forced into the mouth, . . .

so that the victim was obliged to keep his mouth open, being quite unable to move his jaws."[2] The accused was thrown into jail, remaining there until the day of the trial, which could be many months away.

People accused of heresy were tried in a chamber of the Holy House, or Holy Office, of the Inquisition. They would be brought before a long table at one end of a dark room, lit only with a few candles. Behind the table sat the Inquisitors, dressed in black robes with white hoods. According to Torquemada's instructions, the Inquisitors presented the evidence against an

An Inquisitional trial could be very intimidating. The accused, standing in the middle in chains, faces his many Inquisitors.

accused heretic, who was not permitted to see it or know who had made the accusations. In the past, the Inquisition had withheld the names of accusers only if they seemed to be in danger from the accused or his friends. Torquemada made withholding the names of the accusers a routine part of the Spanish Inquisition. This made witnesses more eager to testify. His biographer, Rafael Sabatini, calls this practice "beyond a doubt one of the most monstrously unjust features" of the Spanish Inquisition, because there was no way to prevent accusers from lying.[3] They would never have to confront the accused. "The records of the Inquisition," historian Henry Kamen wrote,

> are full of instances where neighbors denounced neighbors, friends denounced friends, and members of the same family denounced each other. . . . Many of these cases would have arisen through sheer malice or hatred. Vengeful witnesses had everything on their side: . . . their identity was always kept secret; and the costs of prosecution were borne not by them but by the [Inquisition].[4]

While these methods may seem brutal, the work of Torquemada was praised by Pope Sixtus IV in Rome.

Torture and the Spanish Inquisition

Once they were arrested, accused heretics might admit their sins and ask to become true Catholics again. The Inquisitors might agree, provided that the heretics turned in others who were also guilty of heresy. But some heretics might still refuse to admit anything, and they would receive further punishments.

The Inquisition used various methods to elicit confessions from its victims. If an accused heretic refused to admit wrongdoing during questioning by the Inquisitors, he or she would be returned to prison. Then the Inquisitors might send one of their own staff into the prison cell, masquerading as a heretic. He would begin talking to the prisoner and try to get him or her to talk about having committed heresy.

If this approach proved unsuccessful, the Inquisitors would resort to torture. Torture had been part of the Inquisition in the past. But historian Jean Plaidy points out that there had been "reluctance" to use it. "It was during the rule of Torquemada that torture became such an important part of the work of the Inquisition."[5] According to Torquemada's instructions, torture could be used routinely to force a heretic to admit his sins.

Several different kinds of torture were used as tools of the Inquisition. A prisoner might be put on the rack. This was a wooden frame on which the heretic's arms and legs were tied and suspended. His limbs were then pulled farther and farther apart, creating tremendous pain, until he confessed.

Another popular method of torture was the hoist. The heretic's hands were tied behind him and he was slowly hoisted up by a rope. Since his arms bore the entire weight of his body, the pain was excruciating. After a few minutes, the heretic would be lowered.

But if he did not confess, he would be hoisted into the air once again.

The water torture was also used by the Inquisition. An accused was tied to a ladder, with his head tilting downward. Iron was put in his mouth to keep it open and a cloth covered it. Then water was poured through the cloth into the accused's mouth. The cloth would slide into his throat, almost choking him.

This drawing depicts the various methods of torture used by the Inquisitors to extract confessions from the accused, including the water torture (center) and the hoist (upper right). Fire (left) was also sometimes used as a torture method.

Torture often proved very effective in eliciting a confession. But some accused heretics still refused to confess their sins and repent. These individuals were sentenced to be burned at the stake.

The Auto-da-Fé

Those who confessed their heresy as well as those suspected heretics who refused to admit their wrong-doing received their sentences in public. The execution of these public sentences was called an *auto-da-fé*, which means "an act of faith." The autos-da-fé became grisly spectacles that brought out large crowds to see the work of the Inquisition. The heretics were paraded in front of the townspeople, holding candles and walking in a procession through the city's streets to the cathedral. All the heretics wore *sanbenitos*. The sanbenito was made of yellow sackcloth with a hole in the top. It fit over the heretic's head like a poncho and was meant to hide his or her shame.

Once the procession had reached the cathedral, the heretics would participate in a church service and listen to a sermon from a priest. Then the list of their names was read aloud and they were expected to do penance. In one case, penance included being stripped to the waist and publicly whipped for the next six Fridays.

Heretics who had not confessed their sins were sentenced to be burned at the stake. Those sentenced to die wore black sanbenitos with wild figures sewn on them, as well as pointed hats. The crimes of the heretics were written on the hats. Since Catholics were forbidden to take human life, the Church decreed that guilty heretics should be left for the government to execute. This practice was called being "abandoned" by the Church. The heretics were "abandoned" to the civil government after the Church had tried but failed to save them from heresy. The accused heretics were then taken to a field to be burned. If they repented before the fires began, they would be strangled to death before being burnt. This avoided the more painful death of burning.

At an auto-da-fé, heretics were judged and burned at the stake. The auto-da-fé depicted here took place in Seville, Spain.

For Torquemada, the auto-da-fé acted as a demonstration of the power of the Inquisitors, spreading terror among the population. It served as a strong incentive for the people to repent of their heresy and turn in relatives or friends who might be heretics. The alternative might be to suffer death at the stake.

The Inquisition in Castile and Aragon

In his efforts to root out heresy, Torquemada turned the Inquisition on Castile. In Toledo, for example, the first auto-da-fé occurred on August 16, 1486. The heretics were taken from prison at six in the morning, wearing their sanbenitos. A rope dangled from the neck of each of the prisoners. They were led through the streets accompanied by Dominican friars. In front of them was the green cross of the Inquisition. At the end of the procession rode the Inquisitors themselves, seated on mules. With them came the banner of the Inquisition—an oval medallion with a green cross and an olive branch and a sword on either side. The olive branch promised mercy for those who repented, while the sword promised death for those who did not. Twenty men and five women went to the stake, among them a former governor of Toledo. Ferdinand and Isabella had given Torquemada a free hand to pursue heretics wherever he might find them. No one was safe, no matter what his or her position in the kingdom.

On May 7, 1487, fourteen men and nine women were burned in Toledo, among them a former priest.

Even those who were dead might be investigated for heresy. If they were found guilty, their descendants were stripped of the property they had inherited. An auto-da-fé was held for deceased heretics from Toledo on May 8, 1487. Another burning, on July 25, 1488, took the lives of twenty men and seventeen women.[6]

While the Inquisition pursued heretics in Castile, Torquemada did not forget about Aragon. Although the Pope had first sent Inquisitors to Aragon in the fourteenth century, there had never been a major effort to root out heretics there. The Aragonese had a long history of individual liberties. They opposed any effort by the Inquisition to take these rights away. However, Torquemada had decided to change this situation, and he had the full support of King Ferdinand.

Torquemada had called together the political and religious leaders of Aragon in 1484. He told them that the Inquisition would be conducted there just as it was in Castile. He began to appoint Inquisitors. Among them were Pedro Arbues de Epila, a priest at the Metropolitan Church of Saragossa, and a Dominican monk, Gaspar Juglar. Many of the people of Aragon, conversos as well as important members of the nobility, opposed the Inquisition. They petitioned Ferdinand to stop Torquemada, but the king paid no attention to this request. The Inquisitors began trying accused heretics. Autos-da-fé were held in May and June 1485.

Meanwhile, one of the Inquisitors, Gaspar Juglar, had died suddenly. He may have been poisoned by his

Confessed heretics were spared their lives and given penance, or punishment, for their crimes against the Church. Here, each confessed heretic has one hand nailed to a post.

enemies. A group of conversos led by Juan Pedro Sanchez then decided to assassinate Pedro Arbues, the second Inquisitor of Aragon. The conspirators hid themselves in the Metropolitan Church on the night of September 15, 1485. They waited for Arbues to enter. Finally, they saw him arrive, holding a candle to light his way. Arbues was fearful that his life might be in danger from the townspeople because he was an Inquisitor. Therefore, he had armed himself with a club and wore armor under his shirt and an armored hat. But it was not enough to protect him. As he knelt in front of the altar, the conspirators struck, stabbing the Inquisitor numerous times. He died two days later.

Torquemada was enraged. He appointed new Inquisitors for Aragon. In the meantime, the conspirators were rounded up and tortured to confess their involvement in the assassination. Autos-da-fé continued in Aragon. Forty-two people were burned at the stake in Saragossa in 1486. The people of Barcelona tried to prevent Torquemada from imposing the Spanish Inquisition on that city. Pope Innocent VIII, who had succeeded Sixtus IV in 1484, ordered them to submit to its power.

The Crusade Against the Moors

While the Inquisition continued, Ferdinand and Isabella were also conducting a campaign to destroy the kingdom of Granada. They wanted to drive the Moors completely out of Spain. Torquemada's effort to cleanse Catholicism of heresy and the Spanish monarchy's war against the Moors were part of the same broad policy. Both were designed to unify the kingdom, strengthen the monarchy, and win a great victory for the Catholic religion.

In 1484, Ferdinand led an army of cavalry and infantry against the Moorish city of Alora. It was located in the kingdom of Granada in southern Spain. The city had been built on a cliff above a river, which meant that storming its walls would be very difficult. But Ferdinand's troops carried huge artillery, which had recently begun to be used in siege warfare. The artillery, which consisted of large iron tubes on carts, hurled heavy balls against the walls of Alora. After only a few days, the city surrendered.

The Moors did not wait passively for all of Granada to fall. They launched counterattacks against the Christian armies. But gradually the Moors were pushed back. In 1485, more of their castles were attacked and occupied by Ferdinand's soldiers. An army of over fifty thousand marched into Granada in 1486, wearing the same cross that the Crusaders had worn during the Middle Ages. This time, they laid siege to Loja in the western part of Granada. Following a fierce battle, it fell on May 28, 1486.

A Moorish palace sits in the Muslim kingdom of Granada in Spain.

As the noose around Granada tightened, Ferdinand and Isabella decided to attack Malaga. This was the port city where the Moorish kingdom received supplies from the Mediterranean Sea. Once again, Ferdinand's artillery blasted the walls of the city. Malaga fell on August 18, 1487, following a siege of more than three months. Soon after marching into the city, Ferdinand and Isabella announced that all the people of Malaga would become slaves. It was an extremely harsh sentence.

The last major city standing in the way of complete conquest of the Moorish kingdom was Granada itself. In April 1491, Ferdinand and Isabella assembled another large army of fifty thousand and began the assault on Granada. The campaign lasted eight months, and the Moors fought desperately to maintain their kingdom. Suffering from lack of food, the city finally surrendered on January 2, 1492.

The victory was hailed throughout Spain. The Moors had finally been driven out. But Torquemada believed that the Spanish peninsula had not yet been cleansed of all its non-Catholics. One more group remained to be banished: the Jews.

Torquemada and the Jews

Torquemada greatly believed that unity could not be achieved in the kingdom unless the Jews were driven out. He was convinced that the Jews persuaded conversos to return to Judaism, undermining the work of the Inquisition. He constantly emphasized to

Ferdinand and Isabella that the Jews, as well as the conversos, must be dealt with harshly.

At first, the king and queen were not persuaded. Jews were successful bankers, craftsmen, teachers, and philosophers who contributed to the economic strength of the kingdom. Wealthy Jews paid heavy taxes that had helped finance the armies that defeated the Moors. Some Jews also served the government as tax collectors and respected royal advisors. Nevertheless, Torquemada persisted in his efforts to eliminate the Jews from Spain.

During the early 1490s, stories began to circulate about Jews who were secretly crucifying Christians or poisoning unsuspecting townspeople. These stories helped Torquemada make a stronger case with Ferdinand and Isabella. Jewish leaders learned that the two monarchs might be starting to weaken under the influence of Torquemada. They met with Ferdinand and Isabella to emphasize how important the Jews were to the kingdom. In addition, they offered to pay thirty thousand ducats, an enormous sum of money at the time, to help pay the cost of the war against the Moors.

Torquemada was outraged. According to one story, he interrupted a meeting between the two monarchs and leading Jews. Holding a cross, he told them: "Judas Iscariot [who betrayed Jesus Christ] sold his master for thirty pieces of silver. . . . Your Highness would sell him anew for thirty thousand; here he is, take him and barter him away." Torquemada then slapped the cross onto the table in front of the king and queen and left the room.[7]

The monarchs finally gave in to Torquemada. On March 31, 1492, Ferdinand and Isabella issued an order expelling the Jews from Spain. Families who had lived on the peninsula for generations were now told that it was no longer their home. They must leave

Source Document

Therefore we . . . resolve to order all the said Jews . . . to quit our kingdoms, and never to return or come back to them. . . . Therefore we command . . . all Jews . . . of whatever age they may be, that live, reside, and dwell in our said kingdoms and dominions . . . that by the end of the month of July next, of the present year 1492, they depart from our said kingdoms and dominions with their sons, daughters, manservants, and Jewish attendants . . . and that they not presume to return to, nor reside therein . . . either as residents, travelers, or in any other manner whatever, [or] they shall incur the penalty of death, and confiscation of all their property to our treasury . . . without further trial, declaration, or sentence.[8]

This proclamation was read throughout Spain in 1492. It details the unconditional expulsion of the Jews by order of Ferdinand and Isabella.

immediately. Many of Spain's most productive citizens were driven out. It is hard to know exactly how many people were affected. Historians believe the numbers ranged from seventy thousand to two hundred thousand.[9] The Jews were forced to sell their homes and businesses quickly at whatever prices they could get for them. Although a few Jews converted to Christianity and were allowed to remain, the vast majority went to Portugal, the Middle East, or North Africa. It was a terrible spectacle as they left Castile and Aragon. "On foot, on horseback, on donkeys, in carts, young and old, . . . healthy and ailing, some dying and some being born, and many falling by the way, they formed forlorn processions toiling onwards in the heat and dust," wrote historian Rafael Sabatini.[10]

The Downfall of Torquemada

Torquemada regarded the expulsion of the Jews as one of his greatest triumphs. Although he received some money as a result of the confiscation of property, which was part of the Inquisition, he did not use it for himself. Instead, he built a monastery at Avila. Some historians believe this may have been an act of self-promotion, rather than a generous gift.

The Inquisition had become too extreme. Many people were being hunted by the Inquisition and unjustly accused of being heretics. Some of them fled Spain and traveled to Rome, where they complained to the pope. In addition, Torquemada had begun to investigate leading Spanish clergymen. Among them was Juan Arias Davila, bishop of Segovia. His dead grandfather, a converso, was accused by the Inquisition of heresy. If his grandfather was found guilty, the bishop would lose his position and his relatives would lose their lands. Bishop Davila wrote to the pope in Rome and traveled there to appeal to a papal court. The judges found no basis for the charge against his grandfather.

This complaint as well as others persuaded Pope Alexander VI, who had succeeded Innocent VIII in 1492, that Torquemada's control over the Inquisition

Source Document

. . . under the first inquisitor-general, Tomás de Torquemada, in the course of fourteen years (1485–1498) at least two thousand Jews were burned. . . . He was so hated that he lived in constant fear of death. . . . When Torquemada went out, he was attended by a bodyguard (Familares) of fifty, and two hundred foot-soldiers, to protect him from assault. . . .[11]

Nineteenth-century German historian Heinrich Graetz describes the precautions Tomas de Torquemada had to take, for fear of being killed by one of the many people who hated him because of the harshness of the Spanish Inquisition.

in Spain must be reduced. Pope Alexander VI decided that at his advanced age—Torquemada was over seventy—the Inquisitor-General needed assistance. Therefore, the pope appointed four clergymen who should be given equal power with Torquemada. Since the Inquisitor-General himself was ill, he lacked the strength to resist the pope. By 1496, he could no longer come to court to visit Ferdinand and Isabella. During the next two years, he suffered from severe illness. On September 16, 1498, Tomas de Torquemada died.

While Torquemada has been credited with playing a key role in uniting Spain, the cost was very high. Historians do not agree on the number of people who went to their deaths while Torquemada was Inquisitor-General. Estimates range from two thousand to almost nine thousand, while thousands more were brutally tortured.[12] Torquemada had set in motion a terrible persecution that would continue long after his death.

Chapter 6

The Growth of the Inquisition

During the early part of the sixteenth century, following the death of Torquemada, the most powerful religious leader in Spain was Gonsalo Ximenes de Cisneros. Born in 1436 near Madrid, Ximenes studied religion and law and eventually entered a Franciscan monastery. Like Torquemada, he lived a strict religious life. Ximenes wore a hair shirt, slept on the floor, and even went off to live in the woods so he could be alone to contemplate God. Ximenes pursued such a simple spiritual life that he provided an example for many other devout Catholics.

Shortly after the conquest of Granada, Queen Isabella chose Ximenes to become her confessor. She also supported his efforts to improve the spiritual life of the Franciscan clergy. In 1495, Ximenes was nominated by Isabella and selected by the pope to become Archbishop of Toledo and Cardinal of Spain.[1]

Following the fall of Granada, the Moors had been permitted by Ferdinand and Isabella to continue practicing Islam. Ximenes, however, decided that this religious freedom must be ended. The cardinal traveled to Granada. In his position as head of the Catholic Church in Spain, he began converting Moors to Christianity. He also turned Islamic mosques into Catholic churches and ordered that books written in Arabic should be burned. The Moors were extremely angry over these actions, which violated their agreements with Ferdinand and Isabella. They murdered two of Ximenes's assistants. A revolt among the Moors broke out in Granada, which threatened Spanish control there. But the Spanish governors in Granada, who were more tolerant of Moorish customs than Ximenes, persuaded the Moorish leaders to end their revolt.

Meanwhile, Ximenes had gone to the court of Ferdinand and Isabella. He tried to persuade them that the Islamic religion must be removed from Spain. The monarchs even seemed prepared to risk another rebellion because they believed Ximenes was right. Because of his upright life and strong commitment to the Catholic faith, he had as much influence over Ferdinand and Isabella as Torquemada had had. Finally, the monarchs decided to offer the Moors a choice: They could either become Catholics or leave Spain. Fifty thousand of them converted to

Catholicism; they were called Moriscos.[2] Others rose in a revolt, but the uprising was brutally put down by the Spanish Army.

Ferdinand and Isabella then ordered the remaining Moors to convert or to sell their property and move out of the country. Most of the Moors became converts to Catholicism. Ximenes had forced almost the same fate on the Moors as Torquemada had forced on the Jews. Both expanded the power of the Catholic Church throughout Spain.

Ximenes as Inquisitor-General

Queen Isabella died in 1504, and King Ferdinand took temporary control of Castile. Three years later, he appointed Ximenes Inquisitor-General. Ximenes replaced a Dominican clergyman named Diego de Deza. Under Deza, the Inquisition had brought a reign of terror to the cities of Spain. In Cordoba, for example, the Inquisitors sent hundreds of people suspected of heresy to prison. These included members of the nobility as well as local government officials who were unjustly accused. Many were brutally tortured and forced to do penance; others were burned at the stake. Some accused heretics, however, were fortunate enough to bribe the Inquisitors and escape their fate.

Under Deza, the Inquisition had become a corrupt organization. Indeed, the situation in Cordoba grew so bad that the townspeople were on the verge of revolt. As historian Jean Plaidy wrote: "Ximenes, for all his

Source Document

1. There should be examination of every town and village in which the Inquisition had not been set up.
2. All persons should be reminded yet again . . . of their duty to pass on to the authorities any information they might discover concerning the suspicious conduct of family, friends, and acquaintances.
3. There should be a search for books, and all persons mentioned in such a way as to place them under suspicion should be arrested.
4. Those who committed blasphemy and such minor sins should not be brought before the Inquisition, for these were not worthy of its attention which should be directed with greater force against heretics.
5. When a person had been [found innocent] it should be necessary for two witnesses to swear responsibility for the [innocent] person's [true belief in the Catholic religion].
6. Those who had been . . . suspected [of heresy], and [renounced their belief in anti-Catholic views], should swear solemnly to have no more communication with heretics but to inform against them.
7. Those who [renounced their belief in anti-Catholic views] after conviction of heresy should also swear to have no more [connection] with heretics and to inform against them.[3]

Author Jean Plaidy describes the seven articles of Diego de Deza's constitution for the Inquisition, originally written in 1500.

harshness, was determined to be just, and hundreds of those who had been imprisoned . . . were set free, for it was proved that many of the accusations brought against them were groundless."[4]

Meanwhile, Ximenes turned his attention outside of Spain. The Moors in North Africa had been launching attacks on Granada from their strongholds in Mazalquivir and Oran in North Africa. In 1505, Ximenes had convinced Ferdinand to capture Mazalquivir, and he had been successful. After becoming Inquisitor-General, Ximenes urged Ferdinand to capture Oran. The king, however, lacked the money to mount another campaign. Eventually, Ximenes agreed to finance it himself from the money he received as a cardinal. He even accompanied the troops as they sailed for Oran and began attacking the town. In 1509, it fell to the Spaniards. The following year, Spanish troops captured other towns in North Africa, including Bugia and Algiers. Soon afterward, Ximenes brought the Inquisition to North Africa.

Opposition to the Inquisition

Within Spain itself there was growing opposition to the power of the Inquisition. In Aragon, with its long history of individual freedom, the Cortes complained that the Inquisitors were trying to gain control of all the courts, religious as well as civil. In addition, the Inquisitors persecuted anyone who dared to disagree with them over the power of the Inquisition.

Eventually, Ferdinand ordered the Inquisitors not to interfere with Spanish judges and to stick only to dealing with heretics. In Toledo, the Cortes also prevailed on Ferdinand to stop the Inquisitors from trying to assert their power over the local courts.

At the same time, a group of conversos tried to convince Ferdinand to change some of the procedures of the Inquisition. They argued that suspected heretics should have the right to know the names of the people who accused them of being guilty of heresy. However, Ximenes stepped in immediately. He persuaded Ferdinand that if witnesses had to reveal their names to the accused, no one would come forward to turn in heretics. Ferdinand agreed, and the rule was not changed.

In 1516, Ferdinand died. He was succeeded by his grandson Charles I. The sixteen-year-old had become monarch of a great empire. Through his family, the Hapsburgs, he inherited not only Spain but vast land holdings in Italy, the Netherlands, and Luxembourg. Charles had not been born in Spain, but in Flanders— an area in the Netherlands. He did not come to Spain for almost two years, while he dealt with issues in other parts of his realm. He left Ximenes in charge of the government. Ximenes was now the most powerful man in Spain. Although he was eighty years old, he continued to lead the Inquisition and pursue heretics vigorously.

When Charles finally took over the government in Spain, the conversos approached the king and tried to

Confessed heretics were sometimes tortured and punished by strangling in front of the townspeople.

persuade him to change the rules of the Inquisition, just as they had attempted with Ferdinand. Ximenes intervened and prevented any changes. Nevertheless, Charles made it clear that he no longer wanted Ximenes's interference. Instead the new king planned to appoint his own councillors. Therefore, Ximenes was dismissed in 1517. He died shortly afterward.

New Directions for the Inquisition

Following the death of Ximenes, the Inquisition continued to expand under King Charles. In Granada, new laws were passed to ensure that the Moriscos were actually practicing Christianity and not reverting to Islam. Those seen keeping Islamic holidays or heard singing Islamic songs were immediately reported to the Spanish authorities. Leading Moriscos gave a large sum of money to King Charles, who agreed to eliminate these laws. Nevertheless, the king did not stand in the way of the Inquisition's being set up in Granada. In 1529, several Moriscos accused of heresy went to the stake.

In the meantime, the Inquisition faced an even greater threat to the purity of Spanish Catholicism: the rise of Protestantism. In 1517, a German monk named Martin Luther published his famous Ninety-five Theses. These writings were aimed at the practice of selling indulgences by the Catholic Church. Catholics who purchased indulgences were not only forgiven for past sins but for future sins that they might commit. Luther protested against this practice, which was used to raise money for building projects by the popes in Rome. In addition, Luther disagreed with other practices of the Catholic Church, including the fact that the Pope should be considered the final authority on all religious issues. He supported the authority of local churches and local clergy. Luther also taught that sincere believers could reach God themselves through the Bible, instead of depending on priests.

Luther's beliefs found wide support among many Christians who were tired of the corruption of the Catholic clergy. Lutheranism also appealed to local rulers in Germany. They wanted to assert their independence from Rome and stop paying taxes to help support the lavish lifestyle of the papacy. In Spain, small groups of Lutherans sprang up in cities like Seville and Valladolid. These Protestants posed a threat to the purity of the Catholic Church in Spain. Therefore, they became targets of the Inquisition, which ordered that all Lutheran writings be burned. During the 1550s, the Inquisition also began burning Protestants. In 1559, for example, Protestants went to the stake in Valladolid and in Seville.

However, historian Henry Kamen has pointed out that in some areas of Spain, the people resisted the power of the Inquisition. In Catalonia, located in eastern Spain, most people refused to turn in family, friends, or neighbors. Barcelona, the major city in Catalonia, had very few prosecutions, as did many smaller communities. Kamen concluded that people of farm towns often rejected the Inquisition.[5]

Martin Luther's ideas proved to be a threat to Catholic Spain. Lutherans—Luther's followers—soon became targets of the Spanish Inquisition.

Philip II and the Inquisition

In 1556, Philip II became king of Spain, after his father, Charles, decided to retire. Philip was a strong believer in the Inquisition as an effective instrument to maintain the purity of the Catholic faith in Spain. Throughout the countryside there were an estimated twenty thousand spies working for the Inquisition who immediately reported any activity that even appeared to be a sign of heresy. The accused heretics were then hauled before the courts of the Inquisition. As a result, many people were afraid of expressing controversial opinions in public because they might be considered heresy. Authors were fearful of writing anything that might be disapproved by the Inquisition. Many new ideas in Europe were often prevented from reaching Spain. In 1545, the Inquisition had drawn up the Spanish Index. This was a list of books written by European authors that were not allowed to be read in Spain because they were heretical. In 1558, the monarchy decreed that any book must be approved by the royal censors before it could be published.

Throughout the country, religious and racial purity became essential for anyone who wanted to hold public office. Not only was an individual expected to be a true Catholic, but he must also prove that there were no conversos in his family background. People with this type of background were considered racially impure. In Toledo, for example, Archbishop Juan Martinez Siliceo ordered that positions in the church would not be given to

Philip II was a strong advocate of the Inquisition. Under his rule books were banned and spies reported information on heretics throughout the kingdom.

men whose fathers or grandfathers had been conversos. In Toledo, as well as in other cities, the racially "impure" were also prevented from serving in the government.

No matter how diligent the Inquisition was in Spain, heresy still flourished in other countries in Europe. Protestantism was winning more and more converts from the Catholic Church. Much of the territory where Protestantism was making gains belonged to the Spanish Empire. Philip II had inherited vast territories from his father, including parts of Italy and the Netherlands. King Charles had already brought the Inquisition to the Netherlands during the 1520s and appointed Francis Van der Hulst to be Inquisitor-General there. The Inquisition there was primarily directed at Lutherans, who were accused of committing heresy. Priests were burned at the stake for becoming Lutheran ministers and getting married. Pregnant Lutheran women were burned. During the 1560s, the people of the Netherlands rose up against the Spanish and began destroying Catholic churches.

The revolt against the Inquisition was part of a massive uprising led by William, Prince of Orange, known as William the Silent. William was protesting not only the actions of the Inquisitors but the efforts by Philip II to restrict the liberties of the Dutch. Philip sent the Duke of Alva to end the revolt. Anyone guilty of opposing the Spanish monarchy or practicing Protestantism was arrested and thrown into prison. Many were hanged or burned at the stake. Nevertheless, in 1581, the northern provinces of the Netherlands were successful in gaining their independence from Spain.

The Inquisition in the Spanish Empire

Not only did Spain have a large empire in Europe, but during the fifteenth and sixteenth centuries, it established an enormous overseas empire in the New World. In 1492, Christopher Columbus had sailed to the Americas and laid claim to territories in San Salvador, Puerto Rico, and Hispaniola for the Spanish crown. The voyages of Columbus were followed by other Spanish conquests. In 1521, Hernán Cortes conquered the mighty Aztec Empire in Mexico. During the 1530s, another conquistador, Francisco Pizarro, and a small band of Spanish horsemen destroyed the large Incan Empire of Peru. These conquests included enormous gold and silver mines, which led to a steady flow of riches from the Americas back to Spain.

The Spanish monarchs were eager to obtain this new wealth. It helped them finance their wars in Europe. They also regarded the Americas as a new territory for spreading the Catholic faith. In 1570, Philip II established the Inquisition in the Spanish Empire overseas. Moya de Contreras became Inquisitor-General for Mexico. In 1574, more than thirty Lutherans were burned at the stake in Mexico. In the same year, the Inquisition was established in Peru, where Servan de Cerezuela was appointed Inquisitor-General. The Inquisitors held their court in Lima, the capital of Peru. A few Protestants were burned at the stake during the 1580s.

While the Inquisition operated successfully in the New World, there were never the number of burnings that occurred in Europe. By the seventeenth century, Protestants avoided the Spanish colonies, so there were few "heretics" to be found there. Instead, Protestants and Jews went to the newly founded American colonies of other nations, such as England and Holland. These colonies often granted greater religious freedom. In Spain, however, only Catholics were permitted to worship. There, the Inquisition remained a feared instrument of persecution and death.

Chapter 7

Power, Decline, and Fall

The Inquisition was a powerful force in Spain for more than three centuries. Under King Philip II, the courts of the Inquisition rounded up Protestant heretics and conversos suspected of heresy. In 1580, Spain conquered Portugal. The families of the Jews who had been expelled from Spain and taken refuge in Portugal now found themselves the victims of terrible persecution. The Inquisition held numerous autos-da-fé. Indeed, conditions became so terrible for the conversos, that many of them returned to Spain. Here they were hounded by the Spanish Inquisition, tortured until they admitted their heresies, or burned at the stake.

During this same period, the Inquisition also focused its attention on Moriscos who might be guilty of secretly practicing their old religion. Many of these suspected heretics who lived in Granada were rounded up by the soldiers of the Inquisition, imprisoned, and tortured to confess their heresy. The Moors resented this persecution. In 1568, they revolted against Philip II. The king brutally suppressed the revolution, killing thousands of Moors and selling many captives into slavery.

Philip II died in 1598, and he was succeeded by his son Philip III. Nevertheless, the persecution of the Moors continued. Between 1575 and 1610, an estimated two hundred Moriscos were burned at the stake for heresy, far more than the number of Protestants.[1] Once again, the Moors planned a revolt. In 1608, they decided to rise up in Valencia, with the help of Islamic troops from North Africa. But the uprising was uncovered and stopped before it could begin. At this point, Philip III decided the time had come to eliminate all Moriscos from Spain, just as Ferdinand and Isabella had banished the Jews.

The expulsion of the Moriscos began in 1609. It continued until 1615, when almost all of them were gone. In 1609, one hundred fifty thousand Moriscos were driven out of Valencia; and the following year, almost sixty-five thousand were forced out of Castile.[2] Like the Jews two decades earlier, the Moriscos were forced to sell their homes and other possessions at cheap prices. They needed to get any money they could as quickly as possible before leaving Spain. The expulsion of the Jews had eliminated many of Spain's leading merchants, bankers,

In 1609, Spain's King Philip III ordered the expulsion of the Moriscos— Moors who had converted to the Christian religion.

teachers, writers, and philosophers. The loss of the Moriscos removed the country's best farmers. The Moriscos had mastered the technique of irrigation, turning much of the dry land of Spain into fertile agricultural fields. As historians R. R. Palmer and Joel Colton wrote: "The Moriscos included some of the best farmers and most skilled [craftsmen] in the country."[3] There was no one to take their place.

Meanwhile, the economy of Spain was declining. Although millions of dollars in gold and silver had been pouring into Spain from the New World, much of it was squandered on costly wars against the English, the Dutch, and the French. To make matters worse, without the Jews and the Moors, Spain lacked its finest farmers, merchants, and artisans. The Spanish nobles did not engage in work, believing it was beneath them. Instead, they lived idly on their estates, off the income from their investments in Spanish America.

The Inquisition Under Philip IV

While the economic decline of Spain continued during the seventeenth century, the power of the Inquisition remained strong. Philip IV became king in 1621. On July 4, 1624, the king and his wife attended an auto-da-fé in Madrid. A stage had been erected for the royal couple and their court, as well as for the high officials of the Inquisition. After the sentences had been handed out to the seven condemned victims, they were burned at the stake. Philip IV was a king who loved celebrations, banquets, and merrymaking. But after enjoying himself, he often felt guilty and knelt in prayer to ask forgiveness from God for his sins. To Philip, the Inquisition was one way he believed he could earn salvation in heaven.

The Inquisition was even more powerful under Philip IV than it had been under Philip II. The reason is that Philip IV was a weaker king and far less interested in running the government than his grandfather, Philip II, had been. Therefore, the Inquisition was given greater freedom to increase its authority. In Aragon, for example, the Cortes complained about the uncontrolled power of the Inquisition. But Philip did nothing to rein in the Inquisitors. He was convinced that large autos-da-fé would preserve the Catholic faith and earn him the gratitude of God. Many of the victims of the Inquisition were conversos. As historian Henry Kamen explained: "The 1650s saw the beginning of wholesale arrests and trials which constituted nothing less than a reign of terror for the Portuguese converso minority in Spain."[4]

Philip IV died in 1665, leaving the throne to his four-year-old son, Charles II. He was known as Charles the Bewitched, because he lacked the intelligence and maturity to rule Spain. Instead he was dominated by his advisors and his mother, Mariana. Once again, the weakness of the government gave increased power to the Inquisition. In 1680, for example, an enormous auto-da-fé occurred in Madrid. Charles and his wife witnessed the burning of more

Autos-da-fé flourished under the reigns of Philip IV and Charles II.

than one hundred people who were found guilty of heresy. Many of them were conversos. Others were burned at Cordoba in 1684.

Charles was incapable of having children. Therefore, he decided that his heir should be a grandson of Louis XIV, the king of France. Louis XIV was related by marriage to the royal house of Spain. He was the grandson of Philip III and had married a daughter of Philip IV. Louis's grandson, the Duke of Anjou, became Philip V in 1700.

The Inquisition Under Philip V

The reign of Philip V marked the beginning of a decline in the power of the Inquisition. When Philip started his rule, an auto-da-fé was held to celebrate the new reign. But Philip did not appear at the event. In France, no institution such as the Inquisition was permitted to have any power that might rival the king's. All power was held in the hands of Louis XIV. His grandson, Philip V, wanted to rule like the king of France. Philip V tried to reduce the authority of the Inquisition in Spain and increase the power of the monarchy. Nevertheless, the Inquisition continued to operate under Philip. Although the king wanted to rein in the power of the Inquisition and not attend autos-da-fé, he was forced to change. "Philip V grew to learn that he must live according to the customs of his subjects," wrote Kamen, "and did not after [the beginning of his reign] refuse to attend *autos*."[5]

Although the Inquisition continued under Philip's successors, Ferdinand VI and Charles III, its power was in decline. In Europe, the eighteenth century was called the Age of Enlightenment. New ideas were constantly being discussed by philosophers, writers, and politicians. In this atmosphere, the Inquisition seemed like a throwback to the past. Spain was now ruled by the same royal house as France, the Bourbons. French philosophers such as Voltaire, Jean Jacques Rousseau, and Charles-Louis de Secondat, Baron de Montesquieu, wrote about radical political and social ideas. Although there was censorship in France, the philosophers were still permitted to publish their writings.

Charles III, who was called the "philosopher king," brought many of these same ideas into Spain. The leaders of the Inquisition now realized that they could no longer engage in arbitrary torture and burning as in the past. As one historian wrote: "The spirit of the age, reflected in the attitude of the Court and the ministers, was too strong for the Inquisition; it no longer possessed the authority and respect that it had hitherto enjoyed. . . ."[6]

In addition, the Inquisition had lost its economic value to the monarchy. In the past, the Inquisitors confiscated the property of heretics, much of which went to the monarchy. During the seventeenth and eighteenth centuries, however, Spain was becoming more impoverished. So the Inquisition no longer provided much economic benefit.

The Inquisition was allowed to continue under Charles III, despite the fact that it was no longer making the monarchy much money. Charles III felt that the Inquisition was the will of the people.

Nevertheless, the Inquisition was not abolished. It had been part of Spanish culture for far too long. As Charles III put it: "The Spaniards want it, and it does not bother me."[7]

The End of the Inquisition

Although the Inquisition was declining, it suddenly sprang back to life during the 1790s because of the French Revolution. When Spaniards saw the overthrow of the Bourbons in France, they feared that a similar event might occur in Spain. The Inquisition represented a strong conservative institution that would protect Spaniards against the radical ideas of the French Revolution. Therefore, the Inquisition continued to operate for another decade. Its major role was to ensure that all pamphlets from France proclaiming political freedom were prevented from circulating in Spain.

However, the days of the Spanish Inquisition were numbered. In 1808, the armies of Napoleon Bonaparte, the emperor of France, overthrew the Spanish government. Napoleon had no patience for the old ideas of the Inquisition. He ordered it to be abolished. Nevertheless, the Inquisition did not die easily. After Napoleon was defeated in 1814 by an alliance of European nations, Ferdinand VII was declared king of Spain. He decided to bring back the Inquisition, declaring that it "was necessary, owing to the evil done to religion by the presence in the country during the [war with France] of so many heretical foreign soldiers."[8]

The Inquisition had such deep roots in Spanish soil that some Spaniards welcomed its return. But others opposed it. They rebelled against the repressive rule of Ferdinand VII and overthrew him in 1820. Eventually, Ferdinand was restored to power in 1823, with the help of a French army that wanted to maintain a monarchy in Spain. But France required Ferdinand to abolish the Inquisition. Nevertheless, heretics still were not entirely safe in Spain. In 1826 a heretic named Cayetano Ripoll was hanged for heresy. Ripoll was the last person to be killed by the Inquisition. In 1834, it was completely abolished.

Chapter 8

The Inquisition in History

Over the centuries, the Spanish Inquisition has become a synonym for cruelty, persecution, and death. Torquemada, Spain's first Inquisitor-General, has been considered a religious zealot who was determined to strengthen Spanish Catholicism, even if it meant burning heretics at the stake.

The Spanish Inquisition was not the first religious organization to persecute heretics. The Catholic Church in Rome had begun an Inquisition several centuries earlier. Heretics were treated harshly, subjected to torture until they confessed their sins, and burned at the stake if they did not. In England, for example, John Wycliffe had been condemned as a heretic in 1380. In 1415, John Huss, a Czech religious reformer, was tried as a heretic and burned. Joan of Arc, the young French heroine who led her armies during the Hundred Years War, was burned for heresy by the Catholic Church in 1431.

During the fifteenth century and afterward, most people were very sincere in their religious beliefs. Heresy was considered a sin that might earn the sinner eternal damnation—being sent to hell to be tortured forever. Heretics also threatened to undermine the established order of society. They called into question the teachings of the Catholic Church—those of the pope, his cardinals, and his bishops. If the religious order were threatened, then the authority of the monarchy might also be questioned and eventually overthrown.

The Inquisition in Spain

In Spain, the central authority had been unstable for almost a thousand years. Since the eighth century, Catholic kings had been fighting against the Moors. They had invaded the Spanish peninsula and established Islam there. Although the power of the Moors was reduced and finally destroyed in 1492, Islamic states remained in nearby North Africa to threaten Spain. Meanwhile there had been little unity among the Catholic kingdoms until the latter part of the fifteenth century, following the marriage of Isabella of Castile to Ferdinand of Aragon. Therefore, the Spanish Inquisition seemed to the two monarchs like a valuable institution to preserve the purity of Catholic Spain and strengthen the power of the monarchy. Many people in Spain supported the Inquisition. They

This painful device used by Inquisitors was called fire-torture by wheel. The accused was tied to an uncomfortable wheel which could be rotated so that the victim's feet would move closer and closer to a fire burning at the bottom.

believed that heretics should be sentenced to death. They also enjoyed the spectacles created by the autos-da-fé. Finally, the Inquisition confiscated the property of condemned heretics, providing an extra source of income for the Spanish throne.

During the sixteenth century, Spanish monarchs became the leaders of a vast crusade to defeat the forces of Protestantism. It had broken out in Germany and spread to other countries. The Inquisition was used as an instrument by the Spanish monarchs in the Netherlands and elsewhere to root out Protestantism. At home, Spain wanted to use the power of the Inquisition to uncover and, if necessary, burn all Protestant heretics.

Spain was not alone in its reaction to heresy. In England, for example, under Queen Mary I, many Protestants were condemned as heretics during the 1550s and went to the stake.

The Cruelty of the Spanish Inquisition

Nevertheless, Spain seemed to go beyond other countries in its treatment of heretics. Torquemada played a key role in convincing Ferdinand and Isabella to expel the conversos in 1492. Jewish refugees were brutally treated by the Spanish, their property confiscated, and their wealth destroyed. As a result, Spain lost many of its most successful merchants, bankers, writers, teachers, and philosophers. Any conversos who returned to Spain were hauled before the Inquisition. Just over a century later, the Moriscos suffered the same fate.

They were treated just as unfairly as the conversos were. As a result, Spain lost its most skilled farmers and craftsmen. The communities of Moriscos and Jews were eliminated in Spain.

The Inquisition did not originate intolerance toward Jews and Muslims in Spain. These attitudes toward Jews and Muslims had already existed in Spanish society during the Middle Ages. Nevertheless, the Inquisition increased this intolerance.

The Inquisition had another terrible impact on Jews and Muslims, as well as on the other people of

Many of the horrors of the Inquisition were put on public display, including torture of accused heretics, punishment of confessed heretics, and executions of those who would not confess.

Spain. People were expected to turn in suspected heretics, even if they were friends or family members. Those brought before the Inquisition were supposed to name others who might be guilty of heresy. The accused were taken from their homes in the dark of night. They were not permitted to confront their accusers. They were often deprived of lawyers, and they were brutally tortured.

Finally, the censorship imposed by the Inquisition prevented Spain from experiencing all the fruits of the European Age of Enlightenment. Spain produced some great writers and artists during this period, such as Miguel de Cervantes, who wrote *Don Quixote*, and Diego de Silva y Velázquez, one of Europe's most famous painters. Nevertheless, Spanish intellectuals were often restricted in what they could say because of their fear of the Inquisition.

Torquemada and the Inquisition may have strengthened the Catholic Church of Spain. Nevertheless, the Spanish paid a terrible price in terms of how much they suffered from fear, persecution, and intolerance.

Persecution of the Jews did not die with the end of the Spanish Inquisition. In the twentieth century, for example, 6 million Jews died during the Holocaust—the mass murder of Jews by the Nazi party in Germany during World War II. The Inquisition's legacy of intolerance and persecution still exists even today.

Timeline

64—Peter crucified in Rome.

303—Christians persecuted under Emperor Diocletian.

312—Emperor Constantine wins battle at the Milvian Bridge, grants religious toleration to Christians.

324—Constantine calls Council of Nicaea.

440—Pope Leo I works to stamp out heresy.
–461

527—Emperor Justinian tries to root out heresy.
–565

632—Death of Muhammad.

637—Muslim armies begin to conquer lands in Middle East and North Africa.

730—Muslims conquer Spain.

1095—Pope Urban II calls First Crusade to recapture Holy Land from Muslims.

1212—Alfonso VIII of Castile wins great victory against Moors at Las Navas de Tolosa.

1217—Dominic Guzman founds the Dominican Order.

1231—Pope Gregory IX establishes the Inquisition.

1248—Christians capture Seville.

1255—Inquisition operates across Europe.

1420—Tomas de Torquemada born near Valladolid, Spain.

1469—Ferdinand of Aragon marries Isabella of Castile and they unite Catholic Spain.

1483—Torquemada becomes Inquisitor-General for Spain.

1484—Torquemada formalizes the rules to operate the Spanish Inquisition.

1486—First auto-da-fé held in Toledo.

1492—Ferdinand and Isabella conquer Granada and drive Moors out of Spain; Torquemada convinces Ferdinand and Isabella to expel Jews from Spain.

1498—Torquemada dies.

1504—Queen Isabella dies.

1507—Ximenes de Cisneros becomes Inquisitor-General.

1516—King Ferdinand dies; Charles I becomes king of Spain.

1517—Martin Luther publishes his arguments against the power of the pope; Protestant Reformation begins.

1536—Inquisition established in Portugal.

1556—Philip II becomes king of Spain.

1580—Philip II conquers Portugal and increases power of Inquisition.

1598—Philip II dies; Philip III becomes king.

1609—Moors expelled from Spain by Philip III.

1621—Philip III dies; Philip IV becomes king; Inquisition becomes more powerful.

1665—Philip IV dies; Charles II becomes king.

1700—Charles II dies; Philip V, the first Bourbon, becomes king; Inquisition begins to decline.

1759—Charles III reduces power of Inquisition.
–1798

1808—Napoleon conquers Spain and orders that Inquisition be abolished.

1814—Inquisition restored after defeat of Napoleon.

1835—Inquisition completely abolished.

Chapter Notes

Chapter 1. Battling Heresy

1. B. Netanyahu, *The Origins of the Inquisition in Fifteenth Century Spain* (New York: Random House, 1995), pp. 1087–1092.

2. Socrates Scholasticus, "Chapter XVI: The Jews commit Another Outrage upon the Christians and are punished," *The Ecclesiastical History*, May 27, 1999, <http://www.ccel.org/fathers2/NPNF2-02/Npnf2-02-12.htm> (March 21, 2002).

3. Erna Paris, *The End of Days* (Amherst, N.Y.: Prometheus Books, 1995), p. 222.

Chapter 2. Origins of the Inquisition

1. Kenneth Scott Latourette, *A History of Christianity* (New York: Harper, 1953), p. 75.

2. Ibid., p. 106.

3. Ibid., p. 92.

4. C. W. Previte-Orton, *The Shorter Cambridge Medieval History*, Volume I (Cambridge, England: Cambridge University Press, 1984), p. 30.

5. Latourette, p. 153.

6. Henry Chadwick, "The Early Christian Community," *The Oxford Illustrated History of Christianity* (Oxford University Press, 1990), p. 61.

7. Latourette, p. 456.

8. David Burr, trans., "Angelo Clareno on an Inquisitional Torture Session," *Medieval Sourcebook*, January 1996, <http://www.fordham.edu/halsall/source/clareno-inq.html> March 19, 2002.

9. Henry Charles Lea, *The Inquisition of the Middle Ages* (New York: The MacMillan Company, 1961), pp. 192, 193.

Chapter 3. Medieval Spain

1. Paul Halsall, "The Jews of Spain and the Visigothic Code, 654–681 CE," *Jewish History Sourcebook*, July 1998, <http://www.fordham.edu/halsall/jewish/jews-visigothic1.html> (March 19, 2002).

2. Jean Plaidy, *The Spanish Inquisition* (London: Robert Hale, 1978), p. 82.

3. Ibid.

4. J. H. Elliott, *Imperial Spain, 1469–1716* (New York: St. Martin's Press, 1964), p. 17.

5. Ibid., p. 20.

6. B. Netanyahu, *The Origins of the Inquisition in Fifteenth Century Spain* (New York: Random House, 1995), p. 1004.

Chapter 4. Torquemada

1. B. Netanyahu, *The Origins of the Inquisition in Fifteenth Century Spain* (New York: Random House, 1995), p. 782.

2. Nancy Rubin, *Isabella of Castile* (New York: St. Martin's Press, 1991), p. 163.

3. Ibid., p. 186.

4. Ibid., p. 187.

5. Jean Plaidy, *The Spanish Inquisition* (London: Robert Hale, 1978), p. 120.

6. Rafael Sabatin, *Torquemada and the Spanish Inquisition* (Boston: Houghton Mifflin, 1924), p. 104.

Chapter 5. Inquisitor-General

1. Nancy Rubin, *Isabella of Castile* (New York: St. Martin's Press, 1991), p. 205.

2. Jean Plaidy, *The Spanish Inquisition* (London: Robert Hale, 1978), p. 139.

3. Rafael Sabatin, *Torquemada and the Spanish Inquisition* (Boston: Houghton Mifflin, 1924), p. 164.

4. Henry Kamen, *The Spanish Inquisition* (New Haven: Yale University Press, 1997), p. 177.

5. Plaidy, pp. 141–142.

6. Henry Kamen, *The Spanish Inquisition* (New York: New American Library, 1965), pp. 186–195.

7. Rubin, pp. 299–300.

8. Erna Paris, *The End of Days* (Amherst, N.Y.: Prometheus Books, 1995), p. 244.

9. Rubin, p. 300.

10. Sabatin, p. 413.

11. Heinrich Graetz, *History of the Jews* (Philadelphia: Jewish Publication Society, 1894), 6 vols., vol. 4, pp. 355–356.

12. Plaidy, p. 207.

Chapter 6. The Growth of the Inquisition

1. Nancy Rubin, *Isabella of Castile* (New York: St. Martin's Press, 1991), pp. 336–341.

2. Henry Kamen, *The Spanish Inquisition* (New York: New American Library, 1965), pp. 104–116.

3. Jean Plaidy, *The Spanish Inquisition* (New York: The Citadel Press, 1967), p. 56.

4. Jean Plaidy, *The Spanish Inquisition* (London: Robert Hale, 1978), p. 249.

5. Kamen, pp. 78–82.

Chapter 7. Power, Decline, and Fall

1. Henry Kamen, *The Spanish Inquisition* (New York: New American Library, 1965), pp. 110–116.

2. R. R. Palmer and Joel Colton, *A History of the Modern World* (New York: Knopf, 1995), p. 113.

3. Ibid.

4. Kamen, p. 221.

5. Ibid., p. 227.

6. Arthur S. Tuberville, *The Spanish Inquisition* (New Haven, Conn.: Archon Books, 1968), p. 211.

7. Kamen, p. 253.

8. Tuberville, p. 215.

Further Reading and Internet Addresses

Books

Bachrach, Deborah. *The Inquisition*. San Diego: Lucent Books, 1995.

Palmer, Martin, Joanne O'Brien, and Elizabeth Breuilly. *Religions of the World: The Illustrated Guide to Origins, Beliefs, Traditions and Festivals*. Ed. Martin E. Marty. New York: Facts on File, 1987.

Stewart, Gail. *Life During the Spanish Inquisition*. San Diego: Lucent Books, 1998.

Internet Addresses

About.com. "The Inquisition in Spain." *Medieval History*. ©2001. <http://historymedren.about.com/cs/spanishinquisition/>.

David W. Koeller. "The Spanish Inquisition 1478–1834." *Western and Central Europe Chronology*. ©1996–1999. <http://campus.northpark.edu/history/WebChron/WestEurope/SpanInqui.html>.

StudyWorld. *The Spanish Inquisition*. ©1996–2001. <http://www.studyworld.com/basementpapers/repce/History/47.htm>.

Index

A

Age of Enlightenment, 96, 104
Albigensians, 26–27
Alexander VI, 74–75
Alfonso VIII, 39
Aragon, 38–43, 51, 56, 66–68, 73,
    80, 93, 100
Arianism, 19–20, 35
Arius, 19
auto-da-fé, 63, 65–66, 68, 90,
    93–95, 102

B

Bonaparte. *See* Napoleon.

C

Castile, 37–38, 40–44, 48–51, 53,
    56–57, 65–66, 73, 78, 91, 100
Catholicism, 35, 37, 63,
    99–100, 104
    beginning, 19–20, 22
    cleansing, 44, 49, 56, 68, 70,
        76–78
    conversion, 52–53, 60, 86, 89, 93
    threats, 24, 83–84, 87–88
Charles I, 81, 83, 86–87
Charles II, 94
Charles III, 96–97
Christianity, 5–6, 8, 10, 23–24,
    35, 71
    conversion, 19–20, 27, 37–39,
        45–48, 50, 52–54, 56, 73, 77,
        83–84
    persecution, 12–13, 15–17
Cisneros, Gonsalo Ximenes de,
    76–78, 80–81, 83
Columbus, Christopher, 88
Commodus, 15

Constantine, 17, 19, 20
Constantinople, 17, 22
conversos, 46–54, 56, 66–67, 71, 74,
    81, 86–87, 90, 94–95, 102–103
Cortes, 39–40, 43, 53, 80–81, 93
Cortes, Hernán, 88
Council of Nicaea, 17, 19
Crusades, 24, 26

D

Decius, 15
de Ocaña, Juan, 6, 10, 11
de Torquemada, Tomas, 6, 8,
    10–12, 47–49, 50–54, 56–61,
    65–66, 68, 70–78, 99, 102, 104
Diocletian, 15
Dominicans, 27–28, 31, 48–51,
    53–54, 65–66

F

Ferdinand of Aragon, 7, 41–44,
    46–47, 51, 53–54, 56, 65–66,
    68–72, 75, 77–78, 80–81, 83,
    91, 100, 102
Ferdinand VIII, 98
Ferdinand VI, 96
Franciscans, 27–28, 50, 76
Franco, Yucé, 6, 8–11
French Revolution, 97

G

García, Benito, 5–6, 8, 10–11
Granada, 39, 47, 51, 68–70, 76–77,
    80, 83, 91
Gregory IX, 28
Gui, Bernard, 31, 58
Guzman, Dominic, 27

H
Hadrian, 15

I
Innocent VIII, 68, 74
Innocent III, 26
Isabella of Castile, 7, 41–44,
    46–47, 49, 51–54, 56, 65, 68,
    70–72, 75–78, 91, 100, 102
Islam, 23–24, 26, 36–39, 47, 77,
    83, 100, 103

J
Joan of Arc, 99–100
Judaism, 5–7, 10, 44–48, 50–54, 56,
    58, 70–73, 78, 89–92, 103–104
Justinian, 22

K
Koran, 23

L
Las Navas de Tolosa, 39
Leo I, 20, 22
Louis XIV, 95
Lutheranism, 84, 87, 89
Luther, Martin, 83–84

M
Maxentius, 17
Mendoza, Don Pedro Gonzalez
    de, 52
Mexico, 88–89
Moors, 37–39, 45, 53, 68–70,
    77–78, 80, 91–92, 100
Moriscos, 78, 83, 90–92, 102–103
Muhammad, 23, 36, 44
Muslim. See Islam.

N
Napoleon, 98
Nicene Creed, 19

O
Order of Friars Preachers. See
    Dominicans.
Origen, 15

P
Peter, Simon, 12–13, 16
Philip V, 95–96

Philip IV, 93, 95
Philip II, 86–91, 93
Philip III, 91, 95
Pilate, Pontius, 12
Pizarro, Francisco, 88
Protestantism, 83–84, 87–91, 102

R
Rome, 12–13, 15–17, 22, 28, 44,
    46, 54, 73–74

S
Saint Sophia, 22
Seville, 38–39, 51, 53–54, 84
Sixtus IV, 51–52, 54, 60, 68
Spain, 6, 8, 10, 12, 23, 34–39, 41,
    45–46, 48–49, 54, 56–57, 68,
    70–73, 75–78, 80–81, 84,
    86–96, 98–100, 103–104
Spanish Index, 86
Spanish Inquisition, 28, 31, 34,
    58–63, 80–81, 93–100, 103–104
    and Jews, 5–6, 8, 11–12, 46,
    50–54, 56, 65–66, 70, 73–74,
    78, 86
    and Moors, 68, 91
    and Protestants, 83–84, 87–88,
    90, 102

T
Torquemada, Tomas de. See de
    Torquemada, Tomas.

U
Urban II, 24

V
Valencia, 38–39, 91
Valerian, 15
Visigoths, 35, 37

W
William the Silent, 88

X
Ximenes de Cisneros, Gonsalo.
    See Cisneros, Gonsalo
    Ximenes de.